# TABLE of CONTENTS

# Introduction

The reader will perhaps anticipate a viable solution to the origin and perhaps function of the North Salem, New Hampshire site once called "Mystery Hill". Later astronomical alignments became apparent to "America's Stonehenge." Be assured that to date no universally accepted answer as to the builders' intent nor culture of the creators has been forthcoming.

However, the text will guide one through the multitude of theories and presumptions expressed and scripted. Goudsward and Stone have strived to present what has been and what are today the elements to a perplexing site on this hilltop.

Geological data is presented to establish basic information as a prelude to the historical events that follow. Also, water navigation routes are outlined for possible travel to the site. Perhaps Dr. Michael A. Persinger's Theory of Tectonic Strain on psychological/physiological concepts may be left to the discretion of the reader and likewise the influence of geological faults in the area.

Further on into the text the reader will encounter provoking existing evidence of features which justify identifying their doctrine of religion and its practice; specifically, the so-called Sacrificial Rock and Speaking Tube from the Oracle Chamber.

The text will explain in detail the construction of the many individual stone structures and their evident utilitarian purposes. Gradually, a realization of compass and parallel alignment elements are incorporated into the overall design of the site as its astronomical relationships become apparent and are useful in specific seasonal sun positions. Thus, it is establishing a primitive "Stonehenge" effect dating media, a basic requirement for the planting and harvest seasons to furnish food for survival.

The "Woodland Age" is an extensive study of Indian culture ranging over a wide area. Clay deposits in the vicinity of the site provided material for pot making. Shards of "Woodland" pottery have been found on the site.

Much has been published about the Pattee family that once owned the site. Numerous accounts are discussed by the authors to resolve misconceptions of the family by diligent research to establish an accurate account of the Pattees. Thus, Goudsward and Stone have realigned the Pattee faction into a common denominator of reality.

After mentioning several abstract and presumptive articles about the site in the 19th century, the authors rationalize them and introduce the era of William Brownell Goodwin with a biography of his life, a most impressive one.

In the last chapter, THE STONE ("STONE?") AGE may qualify because of his forty-five years of dedication to researching the site for the ultimate information as to its origin and function. Into this effort are qualified personnel such as Dr. Barry Fell, epigrapher, Professor Emeritus, Harvard College/University of Edinborough; Dr. David Kelley, geologist, Calgary, CA; James Whittall, Early Sites Research Society, Archaeology Research Director; Frank Glynn, past president, Connecticut Archaeological Society. Their work at the site resulted in some fundamental information, much of which is published here in detail for the first time.

Dr. Louis Winkler, Professor of Archaeology, Pennsylvania State College, in 1998 made an extensive study of the site's astronomical alignments that confirms and adds significantly to it with stone features outside the perimeter of the principal site.

After reading this book, the reader may lie back, close his eyes, ponder its contents and possibly, just possibly, consider if his conclusions are presumably.... possible!!

*Malcolm D. Pearson*

# Preface

For some time I have been bemused by the tempest in the academic teapot, and by the persistent attempts by seemingly respected historians to advance their private theories to the discredit of other respected historians declaiming over the same subject.

The subject, of course, being the Pattee Caves and their origin.

Some held that they were the works of pre-Columbian settlers who used them for all sorts of exotic rituals and other such goings-on. One wonders where the concrete evidence for such a theory came from. Others, with equal disregard for scientific and historical evidence to the contrary, assure us that these caves were the result of the single-handed labor of Jonathan Pattee.

The two opposed viewpoints have been advanced and defended, not with the end to establish historical accuracy, but to discredit the holders of opposing theories. Both sides have called upon their imaginations and feelings of academic infallibility in attempting to prove their points. Their posturing became ridiculous and would have done justice to Jules Verne.

It was only when they attacked the character of Mr. Jonathan Pattee that I, as the historian of the Pattee Family, became concerned with these opposing erudite scolding.

Therefore it is with a sincere degree of pleasure that I have read this material on the Pattee Family, the first of its kind I have seen, that has taken into account recorded historical facts as the basis of its findings. I congratulate the authors on their return to the basics of historical and genealogical research in the interests of accuracy.

**Linwood M. Pattee** (1901-1990)
Pattee Family Historian
1 May 1989

*Author's note: The material on the Pattee family included in this book was originally prepared for publication in 1989. Mr. Pattee was kind enough to review the text at that time and write a preface. Because that publication evolved into this book's chapter on the Pattee family, the authors felt Mr. Pattee's notes should also be carried forward.*

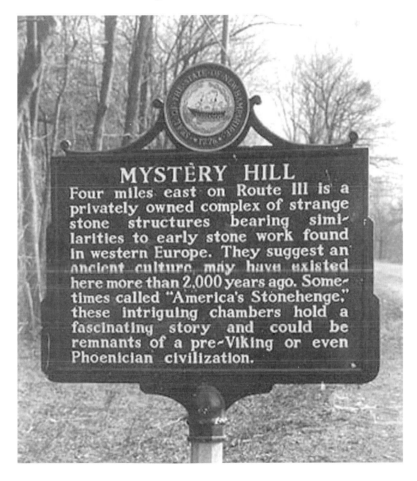

In 1970, Mystery Hill was designated a NH State Historic Site. The marker is located on the east side of NH Route 28, south of its junction with NH Route 111 *(Osborn Stone photo)*

# Chapter 1 - Beginnings

It is the year 2000 BC. It is the early Minoan period in Crete. Sumeric-Akkadian art is at its height. Peru has begun cultivating cotton. Egypt is beginning experiments with ceremonial mummification. Hammurabi is setting down code of law for Babylonia. Britain is in the Bronze Age. The ruling Hsai dynasty introduces a tithe system to China.

It is the year 2000 BC. A flourishing settlement finishes a vast ceremonial calendar of astronomical alignments. It is built entirely of native stone, each monolith carefully hewn into the correct size and shape with only stone tools. What these people called the land is unknown. The land is now called New Hampshire, and the hilltop of stonework is America's Stonehenge.

In 1855, John Spaulding published a collection of legends and oral traditions he gathered from the mountain region of New Hampshire. Nestled among the many tales in this small volume is the following enigmatic account:

> *Years previous to a settlement near these mountains, a hunter brought from thence what was considered by many a vague report of a strange vision seen. He was alone, and what part imagination had to do with what he fancied to be true, judge ye who please. He was camping far up among the White Hills, on a stream called by the natives "Singrawack," one night, when his camp-fire burned low, and a dreamy restlessness mocked his desire to enjoy profound sleep; and to his sight, on a background of deep blue sky, arose the craggy mountain, enlivened by the magic splendor of a moonlit night. The mountain's northern side was hid in its own dark shadow; but silvery moonbeams were glittering upon its pointed rock, and around its top hung a still, thick mist. Above the murmuring of mountain waterfalls rose a strange noise indistinctly; but, being of stout heart, he heeded it not, save as the ominous hoot of some solitary owl, or the lone howl of a hungry wolf, giving zest to his hopeless employment*

*by keeping up his spirits with a rude serenade for the moonlit night. The hunter's nerves were like steel, but a fanciful influence changed the mist to a great stone church, and within this was an altar, where from a sparkling censer rose a curling wreath of incense-smoke, and around it lights dispersed a mellow glow, by which in groups before that altar appeared a tribe of savages kneeling in profound silence. A change came in the wind; a song loud and long rose as a voice-offering to the Great Spirit; then glittering church-spire, church and altar, vanished, and down the steep rock trailed a long line of strange-looking men, in solemn silence. Before all, as borne by some airy sprite, sported a glittering image of silver, which in the deep shadows changed to fairy shape, and, with sparkling wings, disappeared in the rent rocks. A loud laugh of brutal triumph, combined with the strange vision, startled to consciousness the hunter; and, musing on what had passed, he rekindled his fire by the light of morning over the eastern mountains. Another report declares that, not far from the period of which we speak, another hunter was startled from profound sleep in the dead of the night by most hideous screeching, as of a man in the last agonies of extreme torture. At intervals, through the remainder of the night, above the roar of the mountain stream rose strange noises, either through fancy or reality.*

Spaulding does not cite his sources so we must guess as to the time frame and actual location of this event. Could Spaulding have stumbled across a Native American oral tradition describing early rites atop Mystery Hill? Could the agonized scream be a victim on the famed "sacrificial table" that rests amidst the stone ruins that are America's Stonehenge? Could the careful mention sunrise and direction be a vestige of an older time when the solar and lunar alignments that ring the site were not only unforgotten but also still in use?

It depends on whom you ask. The greatest asset of this hill is also its greatest liability - there has been so much damage in the last four millennia that no matter who you believe built the site, there is just enough physical evidence to warrant further investigation along that line. This has produced a spectrum of theories as wide and expansive as the skies that may or may not be charted by the ancient monoliths. The real answer to who built a 12-acre calendar atop a hill in New Hampshire 4000 years ago may never be fully answered, but it hasn't stopped researchers from trying. Historian Norman Totten once referred to this site as "the most important historical site in North America." Totten was referring to his belief that the site was proof of a European settlement in North America 3500 years before Columbus, but regardless of who built this site, it is a mirror upon which reflects the beliefs and historical fancies prevalent in this country at any given time. As an insight into the mindset of America, America's Stonehenge is an invaluable time capsule. Mystery Hill has been a house site, a poor farm, an Underground Railroad stop, a picnic grove, a wood lot, and a state historical site. Advocates of Phoenician, Maltese, Norse, Irish, and Celtic colonization all claim it as proof. It has been branded a fraud and a hoax. Various Atlantean, European, extraterrestrial, pagan, alchemical, colonial, and Native American origins have been assigned to it.

At the risk of offending any of the proponents of the above theories, somebody must be wrong. However, no matter how absurd or trivial a theory may seem, it adds a new facet and a new perspective to research. A good example of this is William Goodwin's Irish Culdee monk theory, which will be discussed later on in detail. Goodwin's theory of a 9th century Christian monastery was out of favor long before radiocarbon dating proved the monks were 2100 years too recent to be possible builders, but his work on the site uncovered the speaking tube that runs from the oracle chamber to the sacrificial table. This ceremonial aspect of the site might still be undiscovered if Goodwin were not specifically looking for ceremonial trappings to prove his theory.

This book will give no definite answers, simply because there aren't any. It will give the readers the opportunity to review the history and research of America's Stonehenge. It will present many of the theories, past and present, and the reasons why they gained prominence or why they are discounted. Perhaps the correct solution is included; perhaps it is lost among the ages of Mystery Hill.

Sacrificial Table - This 4½-ton slab of bedrock granite is a focal point on the site. It has a groove carved into surface that drains liquid off the surface and into a waiting vessel. A speaking tube projects sound from the adjacent Oracle Chamber to an opening beneath the table. *(Robert Stone photo)*

# Chapter 2 - Ice Age

At 10:30 P.M. on Sunday, October 29, 1727, the wrath of God was unleashed on New England. Mystery Hill and Salem were still part of the village of Haverhill, Massachusetts, which reported chimneys collapsed and stonewalls were scattered in all directions. Foot wide fissures shattered the ground in nearby Newbury. Wells went dry, and springs were redirected, throwing sand into the surface. The earthquake and aftershocks lasted for a week, shaking the houses and filling the air with thunder, in spite of frequent fasts and worship by the suddenly devout colonists. The aftershocks reverberated for the better part of the year, with 30 recorded between January and May of 1728. Local clergy also noted a marked increase in baptisms and church attendance.

This was not the first earthquake to strike the area, nor was it the last. Seismic activity was terrorizing the Haverhill colony as early as 1643 with major shocks in 1755 and 1827. To this day, New England remains extremely seismically active, although most of the activity is measurable only by seismograph. The area north of Boston is riddled with faultlines. The fault nearest to Salem, NH is known as the Newbury-Clinton Fault Zone. Branching out from this main fault are hundreds of minor faults, spreading out like tendrils. One such minor fault bisects Mystery Hill. This fault may have two separate areas of significance. First, it offers a point to insert wedges and leverage tools. With such access, it is possible to pry slabs of bedrock up with considerably less effort. Secondly, it means an earth tremor, not a member of the Pattee family, may have dismantled the structures on the hill. Jonathan Pattee may have arrived on the site to find piles of rubble, which he then removed.

The Newbury-Clinton fault zone is not considered active. It is the geologic equivalent of a scar from the tortured past of the rock, and has probably not moved in over one hundred forty million years. However, when the active fault off the coast beneath the Atlantic Ocean moves, the energy travels along the old fault line as well. In the case of the 1727 shock, the quake was at least 6.3 on the Richter scale, and was centered off the coast of Newburyport, only 20 miles away. On the main site, where the faultline is exposed, there is a point at which a quartz vein runs across the faultline. The edges of the quartz vein have shifted in opposite directions, showing the stress that the area was subjected to.

Although rarely discussed, the geology and topology of the site may have played a major role in the decision of where to build. The faultline could have affected the length of stay as well -- it is difficult to maintain control of the population in the midst of an earthquake. The cliffs and the clay left behind by the glaciers attracted Native Americans to the area -- it is possible that the terrain attracted the megalithic builders before them. To make such a decision, it is necessary to know what those early megalithic builders found.

520 million years BP (Before Present), a shallow sea covered New England and New York. Sediment was in the process of becoming shale and sandstone. Early Paleozoic life flourished, and its remains added limestone to the mix. Meanwhile, the tectonic plates that make up the surface of the planet were changing direction, driven by the convection currents of magma upon which the plates float. By 445 million years BP, the plates that would become North America and Europe were on a collision course and the shallow sea between them was beginning to close. By the middle of the Ordovician age, the plates were in contact, but still under great pressure to continue moving. The European plate gave way and the western segment of the plate was driven under the eastern segment of the North American plate. This underthrust slab was subject to such strains that part of it melted. This melted rock forced its way back to the surface as volcanic islands, similar to modern Hawaii. This alleviated part of the pressure in the plates and there was a shift in the direction the plates were moving. Sediment was scraped up from the underthrust slab and driven toward the surface. This material recrystallized in the process, altered by the comparatively low temperature and tremendous pressure.

Sometime between 435 and 375 million years BP, the shallow sea closed up completely and the two plates were part of the super continent known as Pangaea. Pangaea lasted until sometime in the middle of the Triassic Period (200 million BP) when the mantle currents began directing the continents away from each other. By the late Jurassic Period, stress fractures from the separating continents had connected to split the Appalachians down the middle, giving birth to what would become the Atlantic Ocean.

What happened geologically from that point on is conjecture, for the glaciers removed the subsequent deposits, leaving the Silurian and Ordovician age rock exposed on the surface. It is this ancient metamorphic rock that makes up the bedrock of Salem, New Hampshire. The exposed bedrock and the scattered stone are collectively called granite, but this is more a generic term - the bedrock is actually layers of metamorphic schists and gneisses, similar enough in composition to be classified together simply as the "Merrimack group." The schists are finely grained and consist of quartz, biotite and plagioclase. They are well foliated: a geological term that distinguishes rock that splits easily into thin sections. This schist has a purplish-brown color when freshly broken, but quickly weathers to the medium gray color so familiar in stone walls throughout New England.

The other significant geological ingredient in the Mystery Hill puzzle is the geologic equivalent of a blood blister - a pluton. Newer igneous rock has forced it way to the surface through weakened spots, creating pockets of rock of different composition. One such pluton borders on Mystery Hill. Named after the lake that covers a quarter of it, the Island Pond Pluton is elliptically shaped, running diagonally northeast. Roughly 3 miles long by 1 mile wide, the southernmost tip ends on the side of Mystery Hill. It is one in a series of plutons that riddle southeastern New Hampshire known collectively as the Hillsboro plutonic series. These intrusions are from the Pennsylvanian period, 286-307 million years BP. The Island Pond pluton is composed of porphyritic quartz monzonite, a greenish-gray rock with coarse grain and only moderate foliation. Analysis of a rock sample from near the base of the hill shows the composition to include traces of magnetite. This pluton's gradual arrival would be the last significant modification for some time.

Erosion, weathering, earthquakes, soil accumulation occurred, but nothing to drastically change the terrain. This all changed 500,000 years ago when the glaciers came.

Four times, the glaciers inexorably bore down across Mystery Hill, scouring the terrain and reshaping the contours. The first glacial advance began in the Pleistocene Epoch, about 500,000 years ago. The final glaciation, in the Wisconsin Glacial Stage, was a mere 70,000 years ago. The soil was the first to go as the mile thick ice sheet bulldozed away anything in its path. Boulders picked up along the base of the moving ice sheet acted like a giant abrasive, cutting grooves into the bedrock even as accompanying sand and clays smoothed the surfaces. The rock ground against itself and the ice, breaking into smaller pieces, then fine powder. The gouges are evident both on the site and throughout the Merrimack Valley. These grooves also show the direction of the ice as it moved northwest to southeast across the area.

About 18,000 years ago the ice stopped moving entirely and within 3,000 years was slowly retreating. As the runoff from the glacier increased, so did the debris carried by the current. Eventually this soil and rock blocked the Merrimack River sufficiently to create a lake. The water filled the Merrimack Valley with water as far north as Plymouth, New Hampshire. This was not a healthy body of water - marine shells in the sediment as far north as Manchester indicate it was brackish and heavy with salt water from the Atlantic. Glacial sediment deposited in this vast lake can be used to determine much additional data. During the spring and summer months, melted ice brought vast amounts of clay, sand, and gravel into the lake. The fine sand, silt and clay remained suspended in the water and was distributed over a wider area than the gravel and heavier sand. The silt and sand began to settle quickly, but the clay could remain suspended for months. During the winter, little ice melts, and little water was produced, bringing little sediment into the lake. The only material collecting on the bottom was the suspended clay. Thus, the alternate layers of sand and clay represent a year's accumulation. These paired, or varved layers can be counted, similar to the manner tree rings can be used to determine age. In the 1920's, the American Geographical Society launched a study of the clay varves in the river valleys of New England, tracing 4000 years of receding glaciers.

10,000 years ago, New England was free of ice. The land, even today, is still rebounding from the massive weight of the ice sheet, the adjustments partially to blame for the frequent tremors that rock the area. As the rebound tilted the land southeastward, Merrimack Lake burst out and cut a new channel to the sea, creating the sharp curve of the river as seen today. Prior to this, the river ran south, emptying into the sea near Boston. Based on the elevations at which marine clay deposits are found, sea levels were 200 feet higher at the end of the glaciation in southeastern New Hampshire. This theory is substantiated by archaeological evidence that has uncovered 8000-year-old Native American campsites along a shoreline 120 feet above current levels.

Water levels are difficult to determine. Water was removed from the oceans and stored in the glacial ice. As the amount of ice decreased, sea levels increased. However, the land was also rising as the weight of the ice diminished, with variations depending on the composition of the land. Based on research on both in southern New England and Plum Island near the MA-NH border, we can roughly estimate the water level at Mystery Hill at the time it was built (2000 BC) at 45 feet above current levels.

This allows for some interesting speculation. Suddenly, the submerged rocks in the Merrimack River at the Haverhill-Newbury line no longer are an obstacle to navigation. The Spicket River is deeper as well - it may have been possible to sail from the Atlantic Ocean up the Merrimack River into the Spicket River, literally to the base of Mystery Hill. Island Pond could have reached down along the Spicket River, creating a large body of water that was partially recreated when the Arlington Mill Reservoir was created.

The water level was not the only modification found in the wake of the glacial retreat. The hilltop was stripped bare of soil, with glacial erratic boulders dumped haphazardly. In the valleys, runoff water was trapped; creating swamps in the little soil that was left. The pulverized rock collected and settled to become glacial clay. Beyond the main site, bedrock knobs known as "sheepbacks" were exposed. The top ledge, smoothed by glacial action, has a sheer jagged drop down to the base, which is littered with loose boulders. These cliffs became shelters for wandering Native Americans. The faultline lay exposed on the surface.

Even as the glaciers retreated, life was returning to the region. Mystery Hill, like the surrounding terrain, then experienced a succession of plant types as the environment warmed. Pollen and plant fragments were trapped in the clay varves, and they tell of postglacial New Hampshire. An arctic to subarctic zone was created as the glaciers receded northward. Club moss, sedges, and lichens started the slow process of soil formation, leading the way for laurels, rhododendrons, bearberries, marsh violets, and bearberry willows. As the temperature continued to warm, trees that could tolerate direct sun, such as spruce and pine, took over the terrain.

By 8,000 BP, pine forests dominated the land. The pollen of these newer arrivals was trapped in bogs and swamps, and although site-specific pollen studies have not been made, bogs studied in southern Connecticut, Maine, and Cape Cod allow generalities to be made. These trees produced the partial shade that favored such trees as poplars and oaks. These trees eventually became predominant, and in the subsequent dense shade, maple and hemlock took root. Finally, the mix around the site was similar to the contemporary one. Where plants flourished, so did the animals that fed on them, which in turn brought the carnivores.

Mammoths roamed the original tundra, and their remains have been found in bogs from New Jersey and New York northward. Also wandering the vast tundra were musk oxen. In central Pennsylvania, mammoth remains have been uncovered in a cave used as a den by dire wolves. No remains of these animals have been recovered in the Merrimack Valley, but it is unlikely that the grazing herds could have missed the valley in their wanderings.

Other animals returned with the pines. In one bog study on Martha's Vineyard, over 50% of the wood in some layers show beaver damage. Other animals on the landscape included bear, deer, elk, peccaries, and mastodons. By 9,000 BP, the last component was appearing in the area - man.

What the first human found then was similar to what is here today. The entire area is gently rolling hills, with Mystery Hill being one of the higher elevations at 340 feet above sea level. Other elevations in the area include Gordon Hill (366 feet), Spicket Hill (363 feet) and Zion Hill (260 feet). The area is drained by the Spicket River, which flows north to south beyond the western perimeter of the hill, draining into the Merrimack River. Substantial bodies of water are abundant and nearby-- Canobie Lake, Shadow Lake, Island Pond and Captains Pond. Arlington Mill Reservoir, a major body of water near the site, is not a natural body of water; it was created to supply water for textile mill turbines downstream in Lawrence, Massachusetts.

Once the glaciers retreated and climate stabilized, it became similar to that which exists now. The climate of Salem, New Hampshire is typical of central New England. The Atlantic Ocean's proximity moderates the extremes in heat and cold, and precipitation is spread out fairly evenly across the year (The difference in normal totals between the driest month, February, and the wettest, March, is less than one inch). Normally the ground freezes in November and remains frozen through March. All of these factors may have had an influence on site construction and the ability to maintain a community in the vicinity of Mystery Hill. However, the question may be asked, "Why this particular hill?"

An exciting new theory as to why this hilltop was selected relies heavily on the geology of the site. Dr. Michael A. Persinger of the Behavioral Neuroscience Laboratory originally advanced the hypothesis of Tectonic Strain Theory at Laurentian University in Ontario, Canada. Although his Tectonic Strain Theory was not specifically advanced for archaeological research, the basic tenets remain applicable. According to his theory, mystical/religious experiences are created within the deep structures of the brain's temporal lobe, the amygdaloid and hippocampal complexes. The amygdaloid and hippocampal complexes are parts of the brain that contribute to a sense of "self" in relationship to the concepts of time and space and their limitations. Connections between these deep structures and the overlying cortices allow complex memories and language to control the experience for good or bad, depending on personal frame of reference.

As an example, connections to the dorsomedial portion of the thalamus and orbital front lobes allow the perception of time distortions, such as your life passing before your eyes, or the viewing of eternity in a split second. The hippocampal function could be changed, affecting memory reference -- creating new memories that are remembered as if real, or the conviction that something meaningful and deeply personal has transpired.

The effect is created by transient electrical displays in the temporal lobe. These temporal lobe transients, or TLTs, would be the equivalent of a microseizure. Context and frame of reference influence the details of the experience. The more brain structures affected by the TLT, the more complex the responses afterwards, including a sense of divine guidance, diary writing, or dominating religiosity. Less severe displays include deja vu, recurring vivid dreams, memory blanks, and distortions in the serial order of events (precognition).

The more intense the cause of the TLT is, the more complex and vivid the experience. The cause could be self-induced, accidentally or deliberately. The accidental triggers include fatigue, changes in the sleep cycles, intense pain, isolation or stress. Deliberate causes include fasting, mountain top meditations, or psychedelic drugs. TLTs may also be triggered by external causes. One such external stimulus is environmental in origin - transient geophysical fields (TGF).

A TGF is a very brief, very localized change in the electromagnetic and/or gravity field of a location produced by changing tectonic stresses in the earth's crust and regulated by piezoelectricity. Certain crystals produce electric voltage when they are subjected to pressure – a phenomena known as piezoelectricity. When these crystals, such as quartz, are compressed in certain directions, electric polarization and corresponding voltage are induced due to the displacement of charged atoms along the same axis. This voltage is directly proportional to the amount of strain and changes polarity when an elongation replaces the compression.

Tectonic pressure compresses and stretches the earth's crust, which results in an electromagnetic discharge. These electromagnetic bursts can also encompass visible energy wavelengths, resulting in "earthquake lights." These glowing balls are normally associated with the aftermath of an earthquake, which is tectonic strain beyond the crust's ability to compensate.

Visible or not, the exposure of the human brain to the electromagnetic radiation will be noticed. The electromagnetic field stimulates the observer's brain, triggering a TLT, which the brain interprets as an aforementioned psychological response, reinforced by personal history.

So, the observer has a vision - sudden physical and emotional changes that he may connect to the sanctity of the site. If it occurs once, it is a personal vision. If it happens on enough occasions to enough people, a sacred site is born.

America's Stonehenge, with its astronomical alignments, sits on a fault, near a swamp. The bedrock is heavily laced with quartz, and a pluton of newer rock with a trace percentage of magnetite ends on the hill. This author has personally experienced strange light phenomena on the site, viewing two distinct white streaks of light simultaneously passing from NE toward

SW just above the treetops. Similarly, the Gungywamp complex in southeastern Connecticut is positioned in a historically active seismic area with quartz and magnetite present. Research there has discovered that powerful negative magnetic anomalies register on a fluxgate magnetometer in the vicinity of several of the stone chambers. An electrostatic voltmeter shows a negative electrical charge peaks over the magnetic anomaly as well. Indian folklore of the Gungywamp region is stocked with luminous ghosts, will-o-wisps, and unusual apparitions.

Findings from other organizations seem to support Persinger's Tectonic Strain Theory. One group, Vestigia, has explored the causes of "ghost lights," lights of unknown origin that seem associated with power lines and railroad tracks. Their findings are similar to Persinger's results. Vestigia researchers theorize that the "ghost lights" are caused by stress in quartz bearing rock creating electrostatic charges. These charges would be more pronounced during high tides, when the moon's pull increases the stress factor. If the field is created close enough to the surface, part of the field would extend above the surface. If this occurred near a fault line or loosely packed alluvial soil, radon gas would be emitted into the air. The gas would in turn create ionized pockets of air, enhanced by the electrical field, which gives birth to the "ghost light."

One group takes Persinger's theory even further is the Dragon Project. Founded in 1977, it is primarily interested in sacred sites in England, and has uncovered some fairly interesting results. The Project monitors various megalithic sites in Britain, and has found that certain sites, such as Rollright Stones (NW of Oxford), seem to sporadically emit signals in the ultrasound range. Odd radio signals have been detected at some sites and infrared photography has captured an apparent haze above one of the standing stone at Rollright. More importantly, the Dragon Project has found that there are some unusual magnetic phenomena associated with the megalithic sites. Geomagnetic levels within some of the stone circles were found to be significantly lower than those of the surrounding countryside, and some specific stones seemed to magnetically pulse. Since 1988, Dragon Project founder Paul Devereux has been checking prehistoric sites across Britain. He believes the megalithic builders of that country specifically used magnetic stone in the design and construction of the sites. Sites have been identified where only one stone is magnetic, and that stone is associated with an astronomical alignment. Devereux proposes that the megalithic builders were able to detect the subtle shifts in electromagnetic fields and deliberately chose locations to enhance the phenomena. He notes that all of the English and Welsh stone circles are within a mile of a fault, and such diverse sites as Althing in Iceland, Ohio's Serpent Mound, and the Oracle at Delphi are all associated with faults. The Dragon Project has tested sites in England for everything from ultrasound to radioactivity, and the inclination of their research is that these sites not only utilize natural variations on the earth's field, but also are constructed to magnify and/or utilize the effect. They have found, for instance, that during the lunar or Metonic cycle at the Easter Aquorthies site in Scotland, the radiation level within the stone circle fluctuates from the normal background count outside the ring at the time of moonset on the major lunar standstill. Devereux hypothesizes that granite was used, not because of its availability, but due to its natural radioactivity. His theory is that the electromagnetic-radioactive phenomena was utilized for healing and producing altered states of minds, and that modern man suffers from a form of cultural amnesia regarding geomantic energies enveloping the earth.

Tectonic Strain Theory is just one strong indication that the geologic features at America's Stonehenge are not coincidental. The features are too easily incorporated into the site design to have been happenstance. The foliation of the schists allow the slabs needed for construction to be pried up cleanly and comparatively easily, and the fault allows access to an edge for leverage when prying out the slabs. The elevation is slightly lower than the hills on the horizon, creating clear sighting lines for the major component of the site - the astronomical calendar.

Whether the original builders utilized them or not, there are glacial clay deposits left behind from the last glacier - the local Native Americans knew of and used them. The damage of those glaciers was severe enough that even today, there is bedrock still exposed. When the megalithic builders arrived, the hill would be a bare knob of granite above swampy woods.

Thus the stage was set. Onto this stage came those whose purpose remains unfathomed, their origins unknown, their demise undetected, and to the severest critics of America' Stonehenge, whose very existence remains questioned - the "Megalithic Builders."

The straight edge of the exposed faultline, pictured here in the Megaron Area, gave easy access for prying slabs of bedrock out during construction. (*David Goudsward photo*)

# Chapter 3 - Megalithic Age

They came to Mystery Hill 4000 years ago, strangers skilled in stonework and astronomy. Why they came is unknown, as is where they came from or why they left. The only certainties are the structures and worked stone they left. They will simply, for the time being, be called the "Megalith Builders."

When these people came, America's Stonehenge was a bare granite knoll, surrounded by swamps with pockets of soil and vegetation. Consequently, the site's appearance today is no longer that of the site visited 4000 years ago - there were no trees yet growing on Mystery Hill in 2000 BC. No trees meant that there was an unobstructed view of the horizon from the summit, and an unobstructed horizon was vital to the construction and utilization of the standing stones that made up the calendar.

By itself, the clear hill would not attract the Megalith Builders, but it would be an added bonus to the choice. The ease with which slabs of stone could be pried up to use in construction, due to the previously discussed faultline and rock composition, had to be a deciding factor. Because the hill is lower in elevation than the surrounding hills, aligning the calendar stones with the horizon was easier. This had to be a factor. Also a consideration had to be the ability of the neighboring Spicket River to support a village, near enough to be close to the sacred site but not so near as to taint the hill by living on it. For these reasons, or perhaps for reasons yet unfathomed, the decision was made that this would be the place.

There have been comparatively few artifacts found on the hilltop, especially when you realize the calendar aspect of the site encompasses 12 acres. This is probably for the same reason few artifacts are found surrounding a church - people are careful to avoid dumping their trash around a location they consider sacred. This is part of the reason that theories about the construction of America's Stonehenge start with the assumption that the site's function was strictly ceremonial.

It is possible to theorize such a ceremonial use for the site based on the existing ruins. The following example is just one of the possible premises based on the remaining evidence:

*The summer has passed quickly, and the crops appear full and healthy. There is a hint of a chill in the air at night. Is it time for harvest, the people wonder, or is it merely the weather of this new land. Picked too soon, the crops will not be of quality and quantity to last the winter. Picked too late, the crops will wither, edible only to insects and wildlife. Then, from the hilltop, comes the signal to come and hear the wisdom of the priests. As the afternoon wanes, the population begins to gather around the paths, an acolyte keeping sentry to prevent early ascension of the hill. At the appropriate time, the acolyte begins the procession up the double walled path, slowly heading up the hill. The path climbs then drops down by the lower well. Because the glen is both swampy and protected, fog has begun to roll across the path. The group arrives at the entrance, awaiting the arrival of the group coming up the other path. Once the people are together, they proceed to the viewing area. The people watch as the sun sets behind the stone that marks the occasion, and then turn to the sacrificial table. The bare hill gives up its heat quickly as evening arrives, the priests solemnly repeating the incantations. As the sky darkens and the fog thickens, the priests make the sacrifice. Blood drains from the animal, steam rising in the chilled air as it collects in the runnel surrounding the table, dripping down into a chalice placed to gather the sanctified blood.*

*Suddenly, the voice of a god is heard echoing from the sacrifice lying on the table! It warns that the days will continue to shorten and it will now grow cold as well - now is the time to begin the harvest and preparations for winter. The next time the priests summon the people, the god warns, the village must be ready for winter. In the meanwhile, all should continue to be faithful to the gods*

*and follow the divinely inspired truth of the priests. With
this parting wisdom, the oracle falls silent and the crowds
are ushered to the village.*

If you look at a map of the site, you will notice narrow
stone wall paths lead to the main site from the northwest and
southeast directions. Both of these double walled paths contain
stones that are components in the astronomical calendar and
both end within the main site. Both of these walls head off toward what would be logical settlement locations, suggesting
they are the ceremonial entrance corridors. The northwestern
path heads toward the Spicket River, with running water, fish
and game. The southeast path heads down into a swale, rich
wetlands ideal for cultivation. This swale is interesting in that it
has been used by every culture that has used America's Stonehenge. Not only does the megalith builders' path lead to it; one
of the major Native American foot trails parallels it. The colonists later utilized this Native American trail as a post road.
When the turnpike or toll road was introduced into the area, a
more direct path to the Londonderry Turnpike circumvented
this section of the post road. This stretch of abandoned road
was then used to reach the path leading up to Jonathan Pattee's
homestead on the site, and then as a northward trail on the Underground Railroad. To this day, the path is evident in the
woods.

The beginning of the site tour of a visitor to Mystery Hill
begins where the southwestern double-walled path ends - at a
small structure known as the "Watch House." The structure is
built with a glacial erratic boulder as one wall, and is too small
for any storage or housing functions. It is theorized that it is a
shelter for a sentry, or an acolyte who would lead the inhabi-
tants up the processional path to the site for religious ceremonies. Although it has been excavated numerous times (in 1955,
1959, 1969 and 1981) by independent research organizations,
no clues have ever been found to suggest its function.

The double-walled path serves a dual purpose; it leads up to
the main site, and the some of the stones that comprise these

walls contain components of the astronomical calendar. Of particular note are stones in the southwestern wall that mark the sunrise of the winter solstice sunrise, November 1 (Samhain) and February 1 (Imbolc). Stones in the northeast path include markers for the summer solstice and August 1 (Lammas) sunsets and an alignment in the lunar cycle.

The area of the site where the two paths converge is unfortunately also the area where the worst damage was done in the 19th century. Subsequently very little information can be gleaned about the original entrance to the site. There is a slab of bedrock resting in this area that has a 90° hole drilled through one edge. If this stone were propped upright, it would bear striking resemblance to gate posts found in Malta. A leather thong could be fed through the hole and then wrapped around the actual gate, creating a primitive hinge. The hole does not appear to have been cut with metal tools like several other marks placed in the neighboring rock. These metal drill marks were left by quarrymen who carried away large quantities of stone at the behest of Seth Jonathan Mallon Pattee. The extent of the stone removal can only be estimated, but the work was of a scope and duration to justify the erecting of a boom post to hoist and move rock. A socket was cut into the bedrock for the butt end of this post, and drill holes for the accompanying guy wires are still evident.

The area that would have been directly inside this entry shows additional damage caused by the quarrymen. When William Goodwin arrived on the site, he found a pile of stone lining the edge of the stone ledge. This pile, especially in light of its proximity to the boom post socket, was probably part of an impromptu platform thrown together by the quarrymen. However, Goodwin interpreted the structure as the remains of a pulpit. This was logical to him, since he theorized that early Christian monks (who would indeed need a pulpit) constructed the site.

If the pulpit was removed, the entryway would lead into the area where most of the stone was removed, an area that has carried such names as the "Megaron Area" and "The Compound." This area has a notch cut out of the bedrock, suggesting a support column once sat there, holding a roof too large to cantilever. This, in turn, suggests a comparatively large structure, possibly a ceremonial preparation area. A 6-8 ton slab now known as "the Mensal Stone" juts into the area at roughly table height, supporting this theory. This slab was pried up from bedrock and is built into what would have been an exterior wall. The entire area is crisscrossed with drainage grooves cut into the bedrock, which still effectively funnel water out of the area. Also of note in this area is that another section of exterior wall had partially collapsed and had been rebuilt, probably by a Pattee, and the difference in craftsmanship is fairly obvious. Any critic of the site who wants to claim Goodwin or Pattee built the majority of the site simply has to look no further than this wall to see how absurd that claim is.

The structure that would have stood here was the largest on the site, and because of its size, most likely collapsed in one of the many earthquakes that have rocked the area. This would have made for a large pile of marketable bedrock slabs that were the bulk of the material hauled off by the quarrymen, who actually did no quarrying per se on the site. Aside from the obvious labor and time savings by going to this pile for stone, it also allowed them to circumvent a quarry tax. This structure was not the only one to be removed - there are partial walls and rejected slabs in the surrounding area to suggest a number of other chambers previously stood. The structures that do remain offer few clues as to their origins, and fewer to their functions.

The area that the Pattee house rested on was a chamber, the chamber being used as a cellar. 1992 excavations in the area show Pattee, probably to prevent collapse, extensively rebuilt one part of the chamber. While the original builders were good, they did not build structures capable of supporting the weight of a farmhouse on top of them. The other portion of the chamber, or a smaller second chamber, escaped the brunt of the house weight only to be used as a storage bin by the Pattees. This small chamber has roof stones that have created speculation as well. One slab, now broken into 2 pieces, has a hole in it. Surrounding the hole is a circular groove. The adjacent slab beyond the circle has another arc. Theories range from a tool-sharpening implement of the Pattees to a megalithic age sun-dial - there is not sufficient evidence to prove or disprove the use of the stone circle. It is interesting to note however that it is in immediate proximity to the Upper Well.

Robert E. Stone excavated the Upper Well or "Well of Crystals" in 1963. The name may be a misnomer, because the structure actually appears to be a stone-lined cistern. The water in the structure may be a later development, or it may be cam-ouflage for what Robert Stone found at the bottom of the 22-foot deep shaft. At the bottom the structure is a naturally occur-ring vertical vein of quartz crystal. The vein is of crystals uni-form in size and of unusual clarity for this part of New Eng-land. While Jonathan Pattee would have no need for such a vein, quartz crystals are a religious and utilitarian component of various ancient cultures as far back as Assyrians and Baby-lonians.

South of the main area is a small chamber called "The Lilac Chamber" after the lilac bushes growing atop it. It is too small to be living quarters, and its limited space also makes it ineffective for storage. This leaves the structure to serve an un-known ceremonial purpose. This theory is supported by it be-ing the only structure with an entrance oriented to the south, and the structure closest to a boulder which fronts a stone wall extension of the true north-south axis of the calendar aspect of the site.

The "East-West Chamber" likewise has directional orienta-tion. In the 1950's, this structure acquired the highly romantic but wildly inaccurate nickname of the "Tomb of Lost Souls." Noting the structure's similarity to European megalithic struc-tures, it was hypothesized that ashes were placed in the larger part of the structure, sealed with a slab, and offerings placed in the smaller opening. It is now believed the chamber was a sec-ondary entryway into the largest extant structure - the "Oracle Chamber," and that the connecting passageway collapsed and filled with soil. The back wall of the "East-West Chamber" is actually a roof slab that has fallen from a horizontal position into a vertical one.

Whether the soil that now fills the section was placed there deliberately by Pattee or as a result of natural accumulation is a matter of conjecture - the subsequent frost action of that soil of the wall is not. Three separate excavation/restorations took place on the wall facing the courtyard area to avert total collapse of the wall. These restorations headed by Master Stone Mason David Stewart-Smith rebuilt the wall only to a status that could be documented with early photographs. The 1980 excavation also netted an added bonus - a hammer stone, the sort of tool used in the original construction. This restoration as with all done under the auspices of the current owners, is documented and photographed at all stages and a mason's mark is placed on the structure to avoid confusion with original work.

The East-West Chamber, had it continued, would have emptied out in what is now the lower component of a two-tiered structure known as the "Sundeck Chamber." I prefer Goodwin's name of the "Double Solar," but either name is based on the observation that of all the structures, it is usually the one in direct sunlight, implying some sort of ceremonial usage. The serious drawback to this hypothesis is twofold. First, since the site had no tree cover at the time of construction, any structure on the site higher than the surrounding ones would have received more sun. Second, earthquakes, Pattee, quarrying and Goodwin's work crew have all been in the vicinity of the structure. Pearson specifically recalls one askew vertical wall that was realigned to stabilize the horizontal slabs. As such, the best thing to do about this structure may be simply to mark it "questionable" and move on to the largest remaining structure - the Oracle Chamber.

The Oracle Chamber is a T shaped chamber with channeled bedrock drains and features which shed some light on our elusive builders. It originally had a single entrance, but to facilitate the flow of traffic through the structure, an exit was added where vandals had previously destroyed an opening, possibly a side window. The north passage ends with a small opening in the roof that functioned as a vent with stone louvers to regulate airflow. This passageway also contains several features that compliment the use of a structure buttressed into the exterior wall - the famed Sacrificial Table. The most intriguing of these is a "speaking tube", a 6-foot, stone lined passageway that carries sound from within the chamber out beneath the Sacrificial Table, creating the oracle for which the chamber is named. The sound bounces off of the stone walls that create the recessed enclosure surrounding the table, disguising the direction the sound came from.

Directly beneath the speaking tube is a cubicle behind the wall, large enough for a person to crawl into and remain completely out of sight. A small opening camouflaged near the floor allows the hidden person a clear view of all activity in the chamber.

The east passageway is made up of two sections of bedrock. The right side is a block weighing about 40 tons that was detached and moved about 5 feet to form the main corridor. Accidentally or by design, an irregularity in the split forms a ledge that functions as a seat. Seated on this lithic chair, you are in direct line of vision with an extremely well-constructed square recess in the wall. A flame placed in this niche would function quite well for meditative or visionary purposes. Just beyond this seat is a simply rendered carving of a running deer or ibex on the wall. First noticed by Malcolm Pearson in the 1930's, it is the first carving found on the site, and is one of two pictographic (as opposed to epigraphic) carvings found. The drain at the end of this passageway is the longest extant on the site. The drain runs 45 ft. underground, with a 90 degree turn cut into the bedrock, ending in a sump pit. The east corridor also ended in a stone flue like the northern passageway; it is this vandalized opening that now functions as the exit.

Photographs of the entryway dating back to 1915 show the entrance was originally covered with roof slabs, rather than open as it is today. These slabs were removed by Roland Wells Robbins, as documented in his 1959 book, *Hidden America*.

Robbins, whose claim to fame was locating the chimney to Thoreau's original cabin on Walden Pond, was not authorized to be on the site, let alone undertake excavations. The current whereabouts of these vandalized slabs remains unknown.

The original opening faced the lower chamber of the Double Solar, suggesting that the design as originally constructed had the East-West Chamber, the Double Solar and the Oracle Chamber as one continuous long passageway running across the site.

While hypotheses about original site design have changed with the theories about who the builders were, the most well recognized and controversial artifact remains a stumbling block to most of them. The 4½-ton granite slab known as the Sacrificial Table is at the geographic center of the site, with the special effects oracular aspect provided by the above mentioned "speaking tube." The ramp surrounding the table provides ample space for viewers, but it is what these spectators would be seeing that remains at the center of the controversy. The table has a channel carved around the perimeter, and a groove leading off the table. Directly below this groove, a notch has been cut into the bedrock floor. Anything in the channel would drain down this groove and drip into a container positioned correctly by the notch.

Unquestionably, the table was designed to facilitate liquid draining off the table - but what liquid? Theories range from grapes to lye, but what makes the discussions interesting is a petroglyph found in Massachusetts in the early 1960's.

It was found on a flat stone, face down, perhaps a fallen standing stone, on a mountain in Shutesbury, Massachusetts. When the stone was moved aside during construction, it was discovered that there was a carving on it. Closer examination revealed that the stone had fallen onto the carved face sometime in the past, obscuring and protecting the carvings. The carving was of a bell shape, similar in outline to the sacrificial table atop Mystery Hill. More exciting was the outline of a man superimposed on it. The figure and the bell shape are carved in similar proportions to that of the sacrificial table with a full-size man lying on it. Beneath the bell shape is a circular carving, again in a proportion suggesting a bowl where the notch beneath the sacrificial table is. It doesn't prove that the slab on Mystery Hill did live up to the sacrificial table name, but it remains a tantalizing clue.

That carving in Shutesbury is located in central Massachusetts, approximately 75 miles due southwest of the site. Interestingly enough, it is also approximately 80 miles due north of the Gungywamp Site, a major megalith site in Connecticut. Gungywamp has no sacrificial table, but it does have astronomical alignments.

The sacrificial table is at the geographic center of America's Stonehenge. The geographic center however is not the astronomical center of the site. The layout of the sacrificial table makes for a poor vantage point to view the horizons. And considering the drop off the edge of the ramp into the table area, it could be downright hazardous, especially after sunset. The center of the site for astronomical alignments is just north of the table. The bedrock that composes the sacrificial table was actually pried up from directly beneath the astronomical center. The symbolism of such a gesture is obvious; it infers that while the calendar was the most sacred aspect of the site, the sacrifice was important enough to use stone from that most sacred spot. The spot where the table slab was removed can be seen to this day directly beneath the viewing platform. This viewing platform was built in 1975 as the alignments were coming to light. The height is estimated, since all traces of the original structures are gone. William Goodwin, in his *Ruins of Great Ireland in New England*, casually mentions removing 2 mounds of rock, rubble and dirt while searching for the quarry site of the table. The only written record of these two structures, possible collapsed chambers, is a highly stylized reconstruction of the entrance to the Oracle Chamber from Goodwin's book. This may appear disastrous at first glance, but it actually helps defuse any claims that Goodwin could have built the calendar. First, the calendar was not on the property he purchased. Had he even suspected it was there, he would have he even suspected it was there, he would have purchased that land as well.

Since the astronomical viewing points were removed so readily, it means that nobody knew there were astronomical aspects to view. Hence, Goodwin, the only contemporary figure on the site with the resources to erect the stones can be eliminated from contention. This leaves only the stones themselves to offer clues as to the calendar builders.

The calendar has two points upon which the various alignments converge. The primary point could have predated the secondary point by many years. The primary point has sufficient points to create a functioning calendar; the secondary alignments could be evidence of a settlement now prospering and wishing to make their ceremonial site more elaborate.

The primary alignment points are the cardinal compass points - north, south, east, and west. In addition to these alignments, there are alignments for the equinox (sunrise and sunset), summer and winter solstice sunrises, and February 1 (Imbolc) sunset. As a demonstration of their skill in astronomy and surveying, the equinox alignments are the east-west alignment as well. This may be an indication that this was the most important of their solar observations. While this does not reveal who build the site, the prominence of these specific few alignments tell how old the culture was.

When mankind began the gradual evolution from nomadic hunter-gatherer into city based societies, there was a point at which food supplies become sufficient enough to create surplus. This surplus means that some people are freed from necessities of survival to create. The subsequent tools and techniques that developed meant that food supplies remained constant. At this point, man began to domesticate animals rather than follow the wildlife. At that point, the husbandman was the most important role in society. Agriculture was still not dominant, and in this transitory phase, the concept of accurately marking time began to become a necessity. Mankind, without diversions or distractions, had two choices at night - sleep or observe the skies. Since the dangers of the time meant watches all night, everybody had a chance to do both.

Consequently, mankind did not take long to realize that the movement of sun, moon and stars was cyclical in nature. When the sun moved to a certain point in the horizon, specific weather patterns followed. Once someone realized that a repeatable cycle was happening, it would have been easy to place markers along the horizon to mark the movement. The perception of the yearly cycle became bilateral - the time when the animals were driven out to graze for the spring/summer and the time when they were returned to the settlement for shelter from the winter. The equinox was a logical place to affix these two dates. Only after farming became the prominent occupation did the division into four seasons take place.

Imbolc, a festival primarily related to Northern and Western European cultures, is a fire festival marking the changing of seasons. It is the start of the spring season, when days begin to lengthen perceptibly. The Vernal Equinox, because it fluctuates year to year with the passage of the sun, is a cosmic holiday, primarily related to Sky Gods. This is as opposed to Imbolc, which would have Earth Goddess ties and a fixed date. Although contemporary calendars mark the Equinox as the first day of spring, it is actually the midpoint of the traditional Spring Season. Likewise the Autumnal Equinox is the midpoint of the season, not the start. It marks the traditional start of the fruit harvest. Just as the Vernal Equinox marks the start of an increase in light, so the autumnal counterpart marks the decrease. The Summer Solstice is also mislabeled on contemporary calendars; it is the traditional midway point of the summer season. The Solstice also has fire elements in its European commemoration. The Mid-Winter Solstice marks the start of major celebrations in most religions. Since days start to grow long again, the symbolism around this day is of solar birth, rebirth and eternal life. Many of the major religions have sun-associated deities born at this time - Horus, Helios, Jesus, Mithras.

The secondary alignment center is not so clear in purpose. Alignments include the summer and winter solstice sunsets and the sunrises and sunsets on November 1 (Samhain), May 1 (Beltane), and August 1 (Lammas). The May 1 sunrise stone is the largest of the monoliths found on the site, suggesting possible ties to Europe, where Lammas was a major pagan holiday.

These two points are not the only place alignments can be viewed. There is a stone wall outside of the main site, the southern edge of which ends on the alignment of the winter solstice sunset. Within this stone wall is a boulder which is also aligned with the winter solstice sunset monolith. However, from this angle, the monolith now functions as a marker for the southern most moonrise in the 18.61-year lunar cycle. At this point in the lunar cycle, the moon reaches extreme declination without any apparent movement for several months, prompting British Astro-archaeologist Alexander Thom to name to the phenomena a "major lunar standstill." The other extreme in the lunar cycle also creates this phenomenon, and the northern standstill is also marked with a boulder. However, this alignment is viewed from the secondary alignment point in the main site. This northern standstill boulder has inspired far more controversy than the southern one because of a feature it alone has of all the alignments discovered to date. Whether it is a deliberate carving or accidental erosion, the northern major standstill alignment stone has the badly weathered, but still identifiable shape of an eye on it.

The minor lunar standstills, where declination is at its minimum, are also marked. The four stones marking these lunar alignments, however, also function on the solar calendar - they are the August 1 and February 1 sunrise and sunset monoliths (Lunar Minor North, and South, respectively). February 1 also happens to be the large erratic that makes up the wall of the Watch House. This multilevel use either indicates an extremely sophisticated design or an incredible coincidence.

In defense of site design being a function of a complex astronomical calculator rather than happenstance, the North Stone is also more than the primary alignment. Although it does indeed mark the north-south line through the site that the majority of the other alignments converge on, it also functions at a chronometer and a design key. The North Stone is a chronometer in that it helps plot the age of the site, based on its alignment to the North Star. The North Star is not a constant in the night sky, but it is the base line from which the alignments on Mystery Hill were calculated. The problem is not in the stars or in the alignments, but in the Earth herself. The Earth is not a perfect circle, and as such has an all but imperceptible wobble in orbit. This phenomenon is called precession, and it basically means that the Earth's polar axis is slowly tracing a circle across the northern sky. It is a slow circle, taking over 24,000 years to a complete revolution. It also means the star that functions as the North Star changes as stars shift around the northern point. The North Star is currently Polaris, and has been since circa 1450 AD when its axis roughly became parallel with the Earth's. Prior to that date, from 1700 BC to 1450 AD, there was no star close enough to Earth's axis to function as North Star. From 3700 BC to 1700 BC however, Thuban (Alpha Draconis) was North Star. Either Thuban or Polaris will work as a North Star, but since Polaris has only been North Star since 1450 AD, it means Thuban was the North Star at the time of construction. This means America's Stonehenge calendar was constructed between 3700 BC to 1700 BC, verified by radiocarbon dating tests.

The design key function of the North Stone is much less passive in its utilization. If you will observe the photograph of the North Stone, you will notice a distinctive design: Two straight sides, two curved sides or shoulders and a rounded tip. The left shoulder is decidedly higher than the right one. The tip has been deliberately shaped to match features on the horizon with which it is aligned, and percussive flaking has expertly shaped the entire stone.

Percussive flaking is a technique of dressing rock by striking it in such a manner as to make flakes of the rock fall off. The larger the tool, the larger the flake and greater the skill needed to keep from shattering the stone being shaped. In the case of Mystery Hill, the tool was another rock, and the expertise of the stonemason was inarguable. The North Stone was scalloped along the exposed edges, the percussive flaking not only used to give the monolith a specific shape, but aesthetic elements as well.

The specific shape of the North Stone reoccurs through out the calendar: Winter Solstice Sunset, Summer Solstice Sunrise and Sunset, February 1 Sunrise, May 1 sunrise and a number of stones whose function have not been determined.

Many more stones are dressed in the percussive flaking technique, in excess of 300. In fact, the only stones that are not dressed and shaped accordingly are the boulders of the equinox sunset. These two boulders however are combined in the alignment with two small standing stones of the North Stone design.

Even the sacrificial table echoes this high shoulder-low shoulder style when seen from above. The Summer Solstice Sunset Monolith actually takes the design to a sophisticated level. When viewed up close, the stone does not appear to have the discussed shape. However, when the stone is observed from the astronomical center, it is being viewed from an oblique angle. At this angle, the stone appears to have the high shoulder-low shoulder design. And in what is surely a bizarre coincidence, the fence that Goodwin had erected around the main site in 1937 also has this same shape.

The end of the Megalithic Age is as wrapped in mystery as the beginning. At some point, a decision was made to leave the site. Evidence suggests both a hasty departure and a well-planned withdrawal - perhaps a foreseen situation that happened faster than expected. The haste is evident in the quarry sites. Stones remained in situ, pried from the bedrock, propped up, partially dressed, and abandoned. Flakes removed from the slabs remain still today where they dropped 4000 years ago. Yet even as the masons left everything where it fell, there is also evidence that the site was carefully closed up before it was evacuated. It was not until 1938 that the speaking tube in the Oracle Chamber was discovered. It had been carefully covered with a stone, camouflaging it from any unauthorized visits to the chamber in the absence of the Megalithic Builders. The question is what sort of situation could force construction to stop dead, literally between swings of the hammer stone, yet leave sufficient time for an orderly sealing of vital components? Was there a surprise attack by hostile neighbors with so few survivors that those few who were left simply packed up and left? An emergency summons from the homeland that mandated immediate return home? Could an early winter storm have taken the unprepared Builders by surprise?

As I said in the first chapter, it depends on who you think the Megalithic Builders were. The only certainties are the uncertainties. Who they were is unknown, so their history is unknown. The purpose is unknown, as is where they came from, or where they went. Abandoned, the site began to collect windblown soil against the many walls and structures. Plants soon followed. Although the main site would never become forest, trees took root wherever they could. Soon trees and shrubs engulfed the entire calendar. The Megalithic Age had ended, but the megaliths remained, bearing witness in stony silence as the next age began around them.

Shutesbury, MA Petroglyph – Carving of a human superimposed on a shape similar to that of the sacrificial table, including a circle roughly coinciding with a notch in the bedrock beneath the table. Carvings to the left on the stone are modern graffiti. *(Malcolm Pearson photo)*

# Chapter 4 - The Woodland Age

It is unknown when Man arrived in the Merrimack Valley, but the earliest record of man in the general area is an archaeological site in the western section of Ipswich, Massachusetts. Dated to 9,000 BP., the Bull Brook site is a campsite of Paleolithic Native Americans called the Fluted Point Hunters. Named for their projectiles, they have been traditionally associated with big game hunters, suggesting they followed the mastodons, caribou and elk into the region. As the climate recovered from the ice age, Man adapted. As tundra changed to woodland, Man adapted. The climate became mild enough to support simple farming, and Man adapted. Through those periods, and into the three phases of the Woodland Period (2000 - 300 BP), the natives slowly evolved from a hunter/gatherer culture toward an agrarian one. How far along this cultural evolution had progressed is now unknown - European contact disrupted the process. However, Squanto and Massasoit taught the Pilgrims how to farm in the poor Massachusetts soil, and the earliest Virginia colonies bought surplus corn from neighboring tribes. This is ample evidence the Algonquins had more knowledge of agriculture than the European colonists did.

There may have been contact between the old and the new worlds prior to Christopher Columbus. If the L'Anse Aux Meadows site in Newfoundland is indeed the Vinland of the Norse sagas, then there was contact in the eleventh century. In 1677, a Franciscan missionary, Father Chrestien le Clercq, reported he had encountered a Micmac tribe on the Quebecois Gaspé Peninsula who had a reverence for the cross. Father le Clercq interviewed a 120-year old member of the tribe who claimed to remember the first arrival of the French, and that the veneration of the cross came from their ancestors, long before the missionaries arrived.

Of course, the official first contact between Europeans and Native Americans was the fabled and much overemphasized 1492 landing of Christopher Columbus, and his subsequent encounter with the Carib tribe. Excluding the minor detail of making every treasure hunter and religious zealot in Europe aware of the unsuspecting natives, this contact had minimal impact - it was an island. It was when the mainland visits started to proliferate that doom was sealed for the New World's indigenous cultures. It started with Cabot's reconnoiters of 1497; by 1583, Sir Humphrey Gilbert had visited the Massachusetts coast with various sundry others close behind him. These Europeans left a devastating trail of wildly virulent disease that the Native Americans had no immunity to. Traffic along the great Indian trails resulted in epidemics that swept the lands, wiping out a percentage of the local populaces estimated as high as 90%. Early explorers reported entire tribes destroyed, villages abandoned. In 1615, as an example, a smallpox epidemic swept through New England. Captain Richard Vines carefully recorded this decimation of the Maine natives as he and his crew safely spent the winter sequestered in their ship at the mouth of the Saco River.

As the population declined, so did the ability to maintain a distinct cultural identity. Survival necessitated combining forces, merging differences in order to survive. By the time anyone had actually thought of observing the cultures as they destroyed them, the survivors were a mere amalgamation of their previous selves. Fortunately, these survivors had one advantage - most of the tribes were Algonquin or Iroquoian speaking, allowing them to communicate as they struggled to survive.

During the period of the earliest English settlements in northern New England, the area was divided among loosely organized Algonquin confederations; The Pokanokets, who under Massasoit befriended the Pilgrims, the Narragansetts, the Pequot-Algonquins, and the Pennacook. Each of these groups included subordinate tribes with separate identities. In the area around Mystery Hill, the principal Pennacook tribes were the Pawtuckets, the Agawam, and the Pentuckets. The economy of these tribes was based on the Merrimack River, which they called Merroh Awke (Strong Place). The preferred settlement was not on the shores of the river, but on the smaller streams and creeks that feed into the Merrimack. These tributaries were ecotonal zones, areas where two or more fauna overlap, and the Native Americans, with a larger number of species readily available, could extend their stay for more than one season. When spring weather came, the natives turned to fishing, hunting and planting in these areas. Visiting traders of other tribes arrived, bearing regional goods for barter, following the well-worn paths used for centuries. There was a vast network of these trails covering New England and beyond, perhaps extending west as far as the Rocky Mountains.

More significantly, a number of major trails ran close to North Salem. The Merrimack-Winnipesaukee Trail began near Lowell, MA and followed the Merrimack River up to Nashua, NH and beyond. This places the trail 6 miles from the site at one point. The two Pentucket Trails both began in Haverhill, MA and led to Great Pond, in Kingston, NH. The southern trail then branched off to Exeter, NH. The northern trail continued on to Epping, NH. Archeologist Chester Price recorded a Native American village near the Little River in Atkinson that was still in use as late as the French & Indian Wars. This village, and the trails to it, was barely 2 miles from the site, and there is still evidence of a trail leading from that area, past the base of Mystery Hill, connecting to the Massabesic Trail. The Massabesic Trail also began in Haverhill, MA, and then ran to Angle Pond, and through Chester and Sandown, NH, reaching Lake Massabesic then heading northward back to the Merrimack. Price places a small Indian Village in Sandown along this trail, less than 5 miles from the site.

When autumn arrived, the villages broke up and the families turned nomadic, following the winter game. The world of the natives was filled with seasonal celebrations - the corn crop maturation in late summer, the harvest in October, the rise of maple sap in late February, corn planting in early June and the first fruit of the season in June. The Iroquois celebrated a mid-winter ceremony of dreams, confessions, and thanksgiving. If the Algonquins also celebrated such a winter solstice ceremony, it allows for a most interesting site origin - Native American.

All of the above celebrations have stones marking sunrises and sunsets. Of course, any agriculturally centered culture would place stones to mark these times, but the theory that natives built the site would actually be more controversial than those suggesting European origin - the current professional dogma is quite adamant the New England Indians did not build in stone.

However, there are several tribes in the northeast who have stories about talking rocks that impart the legends of the people to those who will listen. Typical of these is the rock spirit Gus-Tah-Ote, of several traditional Seneca (Iroquoian) stories from upstate New York. The name "Seneca," is derived from the Mohegan (Algonkin) word A'sinnika, which means "People of the Standing Stone." Unfortunately, this is a direct translation of the name assigned to the Oneidas, not the Senecas. The Oneida Nation got this lithic name because of a legend that said wherever the Oneida people moved, a stone would appear and give directions.

In the first of these, Gus-Tah-Ote tires of merely watching from his great rock cliff, and decides to try being a water spirit. But once in the river, he finds that it becomes more uncontrollable as it rushes to the ocean. Gus-Tah-Ote is unable to free himself, and escapes drowning only by the timely intervention of Sky Woman. Back in his rock, he decides to try become one with the air instead. But great winds arise, and his wings fail him and Gus-Tah-Ote plummets to earth again. Returned to his cliff by Spirit Woman, Gus-Tah-Ote tries again, becoming a spirit of Nature. But the creatures are busy with their young, and the trees all have spirits of their own. They have no time for lonely Rock Spirit intrusions. So at last Gus-Tah-Ote went back to the great cliff at the fork of the river to live. There he sits and broods over what he had seen. The centuries pass, and still Gus-Tah-Ote sits in silence, looking out over the river. He has learned to be content in his life.

The story continues in a later tale involving Poyeshaon, the Orphan Boy. Orphan Boy lived with an old woman that sent him out to hunt for food. He was skilled with bow and arrow, and always brought a string of birds back. On one such hunting trip, deeper in the woods than he had ever gone, he found it necessary to adjust the sinew holding the feather to his arrow. Looking for a place to sit while rebinding the arrow, he found a clearing, and near the center was a high, smooth, flat topped round stone. He went to the stone and sat upon it. He heard a voice say, "Shall I tell you stories?" Poyeshaon looked but saw no one. Again the voice asked, "Shall I tell you stories?" This time, Orphan Boy looked toward the stone, for the voice seemed to come from the very rock itself. A third time the voice asked, and Orphan Boy agreed to listen. He sat in quiet wonder as the stories flowed one after another until the sun began to set. Then the stone said to leave the birds for him and return tomorrow.

That night the old woman was surprised at the few birds Orphan Boy brought home. He had shot only a few on his way back, concentrating on the tales the Rock Spirit had told him. The next day the same thing happened. Poyeshaon offered his string of birds and sat and listened. And again he returned home with few birds.

In the days that followed, Orphan Boy's foster mother became suspicious. She hired a boy who followed Poyeshaon to the East, but the boy too became enthralled by the tales the stone told. Each day they came back to the rock for the story-telling, which seemed to have no end, and each day they left some small offering of thanks. Finally, Orphan Boy's foster mother sent two men to follow the boys into the woods. They too began to listen to the tales of the ancient times told by the stone. Now the stone told Poyeshaon to bring the entire village to hear his tales. When the entire village had assembled, the stone began his stories, and meat and bread were left as gifts. Many days the village assembled to hear the tales, and each time gifts were left for the stone. Finally, the stone announced he had finished his stories. He told the villagers not to forget them. He admonished them to keep the stories and to share them among themselves, and to encourage those that remember the tales best to tell them by offering the storyteller bread and meat. From that time, from the stone, has come all the knowledge of the past that the Senecas have.

Looking at key elements of the this tale, certain parallels can be drawn between the story and the culture at Mystery Hill:

| TALKING STONE | MYSTERY HILL |
|---|---|
| Stone dwells on a cliff at the fork of a river | Site includes glacial cliff near Spicket River, which leads to Merrimack River. |
| Stone has encounter with a powerful river that leads to the sea | Site is near Spicket River, which flows into the Merrimack and then the Atlantic. |
| Stone has encounter in the sky. | Site is high on a bare granite hilltop, with astronomical alignments. |
| Stone dwells among the forest plants and animals. | Area below hill has wide variety of flora and fauna. |
| High, smooth, flat topped stone tells tales of ancient times to those who will listen and offer gifts | Granite altar table positioned to allow large crowds to hear oracles pronounced from speaking tube. Grooved table suggests sacrificial rites. |
| Orphan Boy travels east to the stone. | Site has cardinal compass point orientations. Site is east of Iroquois territory. |

Whether the native culture of the area built the site is conjecture, but they most assuredly knew of the site. Beyond the main site, at the glacial cliffs, Woodland Native Americans stored vessels in the sheltering crevices, possibly as a winter hoard. One of these shallow caves beneath the cliffs collapsed, smashing the pottery into shards and covering them with protective rubble. 1500 years later, in 1960, Robert Stone recovered two of these ancient bowls and part of a stone blade. Soon after, Stone discovered that the most likely source of the clay used in these bowls was located just south of the main site in a wet swale bordering the lower well. William Goodwin noted this area during his work on the site, but he did not pursue the matter.

Had he done so, Goodwin would have discovered what Stone did - part of the reason for the swamp's existence was the deep layer of glacial clay just beneath the surface that prevents water seepage. The proximity of the lower well to the swale suggests it may have been an attempt by one of the various site occupants to draw water out of the swale. Whether this was to collect the water or drain it away from the clay has yet to be determined. In 1969, researchers made another discovery - a large fire pit southwest of the clay deposits that suggests pottery manufacture was made in the immediate vicinity.

Combined with the other facts, it would appear that Woodland Period natives spent part of their time making pottery, literally at the source. The process was simple enough to have been done on the spot. Clay was pounded into a fine powder, and then sifted. Water was added until the clay became pliable. Grit was then kneaded in, either ground quartz and feldspar or plant fiber. This tempering agent was to prevent the pot from cracking during the drying and firing. The base was then shaped by hand, upon which sides were built up by coiling rolled strings of clay. These coils were then blended together to create a solid wall. The interior and exterior walls were smoothed. At this point, any decorative markings were added. The pot was then allowed to dry for several days. A fire was then built which, when it was reduced to glowing embers, the pot was placed in front of. When the pot had browned slightly, it was rolled into the embers and covered with bark and dried plants. When this material had burned away, the pot was fired. The pot was filled with roots and pith that were burned, thus waterproofing the interior as well.

This technique was practiced all over the region; it is the size of the fire pit that is interesting. It has sparked a debate within the research department as to its function. The first theory maintains that the pit was used to produce the grit needed for the pottery, not the actual firing. Had the pottery been fired in that location, there would be shards of broken pottery from failed attempts. The second theory suggests that there was no need for a fire pit to produce grit - ample material was weathering from the quartz veins throughout the bedrock. This theory maintains that the fire pit had to have been for actual firing of the clay - broken pot pieces large enough to be picked up were either ground back into powder for reuse or recovered by one of the picnickers in the early 1900's. The smaller pieces simply eroded back into unrecognizable clay.

Neither theory can be proved, since they rely on a lack of evidence to prove their point. Regardless if used for grit manufacture or for firing pots, this fire pit is larger than would be needed, suggesting manufacture of extra pots for trade purposes.

In 1995, during a series of test pits between the parking area and the visitors' lodge, fire pits and postholes were uncovered, indicating a probable lodge site. Going back to the concept of the hill being in an ecotonal zone, this becomes an ideal spot for Native Americans - a sufficient variety of faunas to camp for several seasons, and a readily available supply of clay. As mentioned above, it was also located near the trails that colonists would later convert to use as roads. It may have been possible for a small settlement to produce extra vessels to use in trade. The final favorable point to the location was the flora. Although the original ecosystem is lost to current researchers from 1920's strip lumbering, there are intriguing hints of the wide variety of edible plants once in the area among the new growth. Certain plants and byproducts available to the natives are still available to consumers - pumpkin, squash, maple syrup, sunflower seeds, blueberries, blackberries, raspberries, grapes, strawberries, whortleberries, walnuts, hickory nuts, chestnuts, apples, pears, cherries, and many others. Goodwin passingly mentions the "remains of an Indian corn field" being due east of the hill.

There are many other plants still growing wild on the site, used by local natives as food or remedies, including acorns, goldenrod, pussywillows, sumac, lobelia (Indian Tobacco), wild carrots (Queen Anne's Lace), milkweed, wintergreen, bloodroot, and Jerusalem Artichokes. Some are no longer recognized as edible. Groundnuts [Apios Tuberosa], which grow throughout New England, have roots that can be roasted or boiled. Groundnuts given to Pilgrims by Native Americans kept them alive during the famine of 1623.

The Woodland Age officially ended 15 November 1642 with the signing of a deed transferring all property rights from the Native Americans to the colonists. It is highly unlikely that Saggahew and Passaquo had any concept of what they were signing; let alone what they were signing away. It is also questionable as to whether or not the two would have even had the authority to sign on behalf of their leader, Passaconnaway. This, of course, was not of any great concern to the colonists. Once a deed was secured, the fate of the native culture was sealed, and the colonists would consider any of their actions legal, at least in their courts.

The Woodland Age officially ended 15 November 1642. In actuality, it was over the moment Columbus set sail.

Early Woodland Pottery (circa 1800-2500 BP). Excavated by Bob Stone in 1959 from cliffs on the western side of Mystery Hill. *(David Goudsward photo)*

Slate hoe or hand axe. Found on the site by William Goodwin's crew in 1930's. *(Malcolm Pearson photo)*

# Chapter 5 – The Pattee Age

It has always been somewhat fashionable in genealogy periodicals to critique the accuracy of old published genealogies that cite "family tradition" as source material. These genealogies have always been published (and probably always will) with the goal of creating dramatic, inspiring, romantic, but rarely accurate, portraits of ancestors. In the case of Peter Patee, this has caused repercussions into other fields of study as well. Among Peter Patee's descendants is one Jonathan Pattee of Salem, NH, a cordwainer (shoemaker) who would be of incidental significance outside of genealogy except for his choice of houselots. Jonathan's house was atop Mystery Hill. This has caused the Pattee family to be scrutinized by a wide variety of interested parties, most of whom have apparently little background in genealogy.

The worst offenders are the skeptics who choose to discredit the antiquity of Mystery Hill by claiming that it is the ruins of a colonial alchemist operation. Their proof is circumstantial - since Peter Patee was the son of Sir William Pattee, he must have shared his father's predilection in the sciences. Jonathan merely lived atop of ruins that had been hidden in the family for 4 generations.

The problem with this theory is that Peter Pattee was **not** William's son. Whether or not Sir William dabbled in alchemy among his other activities as a founding member of the Royal Society is irrelevant to this discussion, but the erroneous claim of Peter Patee being his son is a persistent one. The earliest published account of this paternal link is in a biographical sketch of Asa Pattee in Walter Harriman's **History of Warner, New Hampshire** (1879):

> *Sir William Pattee was physician to Cromwell and King Charles the Second. He was one of the founders of the Royal Society, and was knighted in 1660. He was a copious writer on political history, and Macaulay mentions this fact in his History of England. Peter Pattee, a*

*son of Sir William, was born in Lansdown, England, in
1648. In 1669, on account of certain political notions
which he entertained, he found it necessary to take a
hasty depart from his country. He went to Virginia. After
remaining there a few years, he removed to Haverhill,
Mass. In November, 1677, he took the oath of allegiance
to the Crown. He married in Haverhill, and became the
father of a large family. He built the first mill and established the first ferry in Haverhill, and the ferry retains his
name to this day. Peter Pattee was the grandfather of
Captain Asa, who is mentioned in the above record, who
was born in Haverhill in 1732, and who came to Warner
about the close of the Revolutionary war....*

This incorrect Sir William legend is repeated in several
later genealogical sources. To complicate the picture, a major
History of New Hampshire then merges the English Pattee line
with an entirely different line, the French Pettee. This adds a
new and completely inaccurate notation that Peter Patee was
descended from French Huguenots on the Isle of Jersey.

However, Sir William Petty, as his name is correctly
spelled, can be eliminated unequivocally as the Pattee family
progenitor. William Petty was born in 1623 in the English Village of Romsey in Hampshire County. He married Elizabeth,
the widow of Sir William Fenton, in 1667. The union produced
5 children, the first 2 dying in 1670, followed by Charles
(1672), Henry (1673), and Anne (1675). With no child named
Peter, the link disappears immediately.

Harriman is correct when he mentions a brief sojourn in
Virginia, but he neglects to mention Peter's marriage and the
subsequent birth of Richard Pattee in that settlement. Peter's
subsequent marriage in Haverhill to Sarah Gill of Salisbury,
MA did produce additional children, but not enough to qualify
as a large family by colonial standards. Peter did petition the
annual meeting for permission to build a gristmill, but the motion was "fully and plentifully denied." Even if he had been allowed the mill, it would have been too late to be the first -

Robert Clement had been operating a mill in Haverhill fifty years prior to that date.

Harriman's ferry notes move onto firmer ground. When his History of Warner, NH was published in 1879, the location was still referred to in Haverhill as "Pattee's Ferry" in some sources. The ferry itself, sold by Peter's son Richard and moved upstream, was most assuredly not the first in Haverhill; it seems to have been deliberately placed halfway between 2 other ferries operating simultaneously. A further strike against Harriman is the reference to Captain Asa Pattee being the grandson of Peter Patee. A generation seems to have been lopped off somewhere. Asa would be a great-grandson.

A great deal of research was not put into the biographical sketches in his book; Harriman recorded what was given to him by surviving family members at face value. This is because the family paid a subscription fee to underwrite part of the publication costs.

Embarrassments such as court cases, Peter's being warned out of Haverhill, as well as a controversy over the opening a tavern all were conveniently overlooked. If indeed the Pattee family of Warner was attempting to enhance their genealogical heritage, they went about it the wrong way. Peter Patee, when warned out of town in 1677/78, was noted as being a cordwainer. Peter has no other business ventures operating until the ferry c.1714, which means Peter Patee was the first cordwainer to regularly and consistently ply his trade in Haverhill. Haverhill, by the date of publication of the Warner history, would be well on her way to her title as "Queen Slipper City." As the first shoemaker in a major shoe-manufacturing city, Peter Patee's actual claim to fame could have been far more substantial if the actual facts had been given to Walter Harriman in 1879.

The actual fact is that in November of 1677, Peter Pattee took the Oath of Allegiance in the colony of Haverhill, the first verified record of his presence. Soon after he appeared at the annual meeting of the colony of Haverhill and requested land upon which to settle. The public assembly was surprised; Pattee had been assumed to be an itinerant cordwainer. Not only did the proprietors refuse to grant Pattee any land, they also warned him out of town. This meant that should Pattee, due to age or illness, become unable to support himself, the town would not assume responsibility for his welfare. In fact, towns used to take each other to court to force each other to assume the costs of taking care of the infirm or invalid. Undaunted, Peter Pattee bought some local property, married, raised a family and ran a farm and ferry until his death in 1724.

Of Peter's life prior to 1677, few pieces of documentable evidence have surfaced. A record of Peter as a Salem, MA resident being sent to Maine at the end of the King Philip's War in June 1677 results in his being seriously wounded in the Black Rock campaign. In fact, in several accounts, he is listed among the fatalities. This status as a wounded war veteran helped his cause in Haverhill. Pattee had the Deputy Governor enter the following deposition:

> *Peter Patee having lived neare three years in this country, & bene in service in the warr, & somewhat wounded, & living without offence in the Towne of Haverhill for some space of Time, as I am Informed, I doe allowe him to dwell in the Country. Dated 9th of April 1678. Samuel Symonds, Dep. Govern.*

He arrived from Virginia, based on a Massachusetts court case from March of 1681, in which he is charged with abandoning a wife and child in Virginia. In the course of the trial, Pattee was able to demonstrate he had made numerous attempts to send for his wife, and had received no answer. He was acquitted of the charge, but the record indicates that Peter had a wife and child at the time he came to New England. The November 1677 date for a Haverhill arrival is supplemented by Samuel Symond's 1678 statement concerning Pattee's having lived in the country for near three years, suggesting that Peter arrived in New England circa 1675. This earlier date helps explain Peter's listing as a Salem (MA) resident in June 1677. Salem also becomes a prime suspect as Peter's port of arrival.

Peter's Virginia-born child was Richard Pattee, whose early life is as enigmatic as his father's was. Richard's arrival in Haverhill sometime after 1709 must have been a great surprise to Peter, but even more so to Samuel Pattee, the first son of Peter and his second wife, who immediately forfeited his primogeniture rights. Richard Pattee is confirmed as Peter's son in various land deeds, and is treated as the eldest son is such matters as executor of Peter's will, and taking over the family business (the ferry). Since the births of Peter's children except Richard are recorded in Haverhill records, it is safe to assume that Richard is probably the child from Virginia.

Richard's date of arrival in Haverhill is not known, but can be narrowed down some. Samuel Pattee, Peter's oldest surviving son prior to Richard's arrival, is still active in the role of eldest son as late as 1709 when Haverhill reimburses him for ferry operation expenses. Richard's wife is mentioned in Haverhill First Parish church records as of 1715, suggesting a 1709 to 1715 arrival date.

It is with Richard's son Seth that brings America's Stonehenge into the equation. Seth lived on a 48 acre parcel he had bought in 1734, a parcel that included Mystery Hill. On this property, Seth first built a house, a barn, and then a sawmill down along the Spicket River. The house and barn foundations still exist – the house is within the main site, and the barn is to the south side of the path leading to the winter solstice sunset stone.

Both Seth and his younger brothers Peter and Richard were north of the long disputed state border when Salem, New Hampshire was incorporated in 1750 from Massachusetts. Seth served over the years as a town proprietor, a constable and as a selectman. In 1765, he sold half his land, with barn and house, to his eldest son Jerediah.

This property was the western half of the lands, including the site. Five years later, the eastern half of the property was sold to Seth Pattee, junior.

Seth Pattee, Jr. was a 20-year-old bachelor when he bought the remaining half of his father's property. In 1772, Seth Jr. married Susanna Corliss. He also purchased an additional portion of the land back from his brother Jerediah. Besides including the hilltop with the site, this new portion included Seth Sr.'s house and barn, which Seth Jr. needed as a newlywed. In 1774, he was drawn into the Revolutionary War. He returned from the war in 1777, his health broken. He died in 1779, not living to see the birth of his fourth child. His eldest son, Jonathan, was 6 years old. The next year, Susanna Pattee married Daniel Corliss, a cousin. The four Pattee children moved to their stepfather's farm. The Pattee house was left abandoned.

As soon as he was old enough, Jonathan was apprenticed out to his cousins living on the far side of Salem, bordering on Methuen, Massachusetts. There, Jonathan learned the trade of shoemaking, continuing the family tradition of cordwaining started 5 generations past by Peter Pattee. Jonathan continued to work as a cordwainer on the Methuen border several years after his apprenticeship ended. His cousins had a tavern on a main road that supplied a steady stream of shoe repair jobs. Jonathan also had other reasons to stay on that side of town. On November 19, 1795, Jonathan married Elizabeth Mallon in Methuen. Five months later, Jonathan Pattee, Jr. was born.

By the end of 1801, Jonathan and Betsy had 3 children and another due. They had moved back to the North Salem area and the house they had was insufficient for the growing family. Jonathan had mortgaged the house property to his brother Eliphalet, and sold off what little other land he had. He had an idea where he could find a larger house without a cash outlay. He went to see his mother.

On December 25, 1801, Susanna Corliss relinquished all dower rights to her first husband's estate. This Christmas present gave Jonathan, as eldest son, clear title to Seth Pattee, Jr.'s property, or what was left of it. Much of the property had been sold off in the preceding 20 years, but there was still a 35-acre parcel, and on it was the old homestead. It had been uninhabited for 2 decades, but it still stood. And the house, built by his grandfather, was designed for a large family. By the time Betsy Mallon Pattee was born in June 1802, the old house on the hill was habitable again. In 1804, Jonathan went into business with his brother-in-law, Cadford Mallon. As their joint cordwaining business showed profit, the two began buying and selling small parcels of land. When Cadford died at age 34 in 1806, Jonathan and he had sold off most of their properties.

So, by 1807, things were good for Jonathan Pattee. He had 5 children, a steady cordwaining trade, and was active in community affairs. He was the town tax collector and a town road surveyor. As the stepson of a former town selectman, the son of a revolutionary war hero and the grandson of a founder of the town, he enjoyed a certain social stature. Unfortunately early tax collecting procedures were about to change that.

When Jonathan turned in the final tally for 1807 tax collections, the Town Selectmen found it was less than they had calculated. And since they were essentially autonomous in such matters, the Selectmen decided that Jonathan Pattee owed them the difference between their projected revenues and his actual collections. This was not the first time a town tax collector had been caught in such a dilemma, but in Salem, it was a constant occupational hazard. The Selectmen's resolution of such discrepancies included badgering the tax collector to the point where the beleaguered collector resigned and paid the difference out of pocket or looking the other way when the tax collector padded the next year's collections to make up the difference.

Jonathan apparently stood fast on the amount collected in 1807, and continued his work as the tax collector in 1808 and 1809. In 1809 however, Jonathan reached a point where he felt obligated to settle the issue once and for all. He went on the offensive and filed suit against the Salem Selectmen. Jonathan however, made contingency plans. On August 16, 1809 Jonathan sold his house on Mystery Hill property to his brother-in-law, Kendal Mallon. On August 18 Kendal Mallon sold the property back to Betsey Pattee, removing Jonathan as owner.

Like so many of the early records in this country, the case of Jonathan Pattee vs. the Selectmen has been lost. It is very obvious however, that Jonathan Pattee lost; He disappears from Salem records.

Jonathan, now owing the Town of Salem a considerable sum, left his family on the hill and took odd jobs as he could find them. In the next ten years, he ranged from nearby Methuen and Haverhill out as far as Boston. As his children grew old enough, they joined their father in raising enough money to both support the family and pay off the debt. In 1814, tragedy struck - Jonathan's only son, Jonathan Pattee Jr. died in Boston. Jonathan's last child was born the next year, Seth Jonathan Mallon Pattee - Jonathan Pattee's only surviving son.

All told, Jonathan and Betsey Pattee had nine children, seven daughters and the 2 sons. Because, until an 1883 State mandate, less than half of the population was recorded in the vital records, we don't how many of the daughters survived to adulthood. However, a lack of death records in Gilbert's *History of Salem* and the size of the house infer that most of them lived to adulthood.

By 1820, Jonathan was back home and rebuilding his reputation in Salem. One last misfortune would plague him in 1821 when his brother Stephen, a carpenter who had acquired a good size amount of land, was declared non compos mentis and made a ward of the state.

1821 After Stephen was appointed a ward of the State, things returned to normalcy. Jonathan's oldest daughters, having met beaus in Boston, began marrying and moving away. As more room became available in the house, Jonathan began taking in some of the town paupers. Agreeing to take in the town poor was more than charity; it was a source of income. Prior to construction of a town poorhouse, residents bid for the towns aged and infirm, agreeing to care for their needs for a set price. Finances aside, not just anyone was allowed to assumed responsibility for these widows, orphans and sickly. The very fact that Jonathan, starting in 1829, was a regular participant in the pauper auctions signified that he had regained some of his lost stature among the locals. A local tradition of Salem may suggest a way Jonathan regained his standing in town.

In the summer of 1825, the Maquis de Lafayette was touring Massachusetts and New Hampshire, accompanied by state militia members, French Naval officers, and his private secretary. One of his stops was the Pattee tavern on the Salem, NH - Methuen, MA border, along the road now known as Route 28, owned by one of Jonathan's cousins, Richard Pattee. Lafayette and his escorts arrived at the tavern for dinner a little before noon. However, there is a gap in his itinerary – he arrived at 5:30 for an appearance in East Derry, NH where he was expected at 2:00. Historian and researcher Andrew Rothovius calculates that allowing for 90 minutes for the dinner, and 2 hours for the drive to Derry, there is still a 2-hour unaccounted for gap in Lafayette's schedule, most unusual in the high profile, heavily reported trip. The local tradition is that Lafayette went to view the strange stone ruins on cousin Jonathan's property. It is not entirely out of the question – the route to Derry passes the Old Salem Road, which leads directly to Haverhill Road and the Pattee homestead. A French naval uniform button of the proper age was found on the site in the late 1950's, but this in inconclusive, especially in light on the complete lack of written material to support the story. Still, it is an intriguing local legend.

By 1835, the Pattee house was home to 11 paupers, including Jonathan's brother Stephen Pattee. After being made a ward of the State in 1821, his court appointed guardian sold off all of Stephen's considerable property holdings, to help cover "expenses." Within 10 years, these expenses had drained all of the funds, and Stephen's guardian removed himself from his obligations, leaving Stephen a pauper.

Apparently Jonathan and Betsy, now in their 60's, found the strain caring for that many wards too much. The next year, the paupers on the hill dropped to 8, and by 1838, Jonathan and Betsy no longer cared for paupers. Only Jonathan, his wife and son Seth J.M. remained in the house. Jonathan continued to occasionally work as a cordwainer, but Seth J.M now was old enough to bear the brunt of work around the property.

Seth Jonathan Mallon Pattee married Hannah Nichols in 1840. After living with the Nichols for a few years, Seth, his wife and child returned to the Pattee homestead. Jonathan Pattee died in September of 1849 at the age of 76. When Jonathan's will was not found, he was declared intestate, and Seth J.M., as eldest son, was appointed heir.

Mystery Hill did not fare as well under Seth Jonathan Mallon Pattee as it had under his father. Most of the damage attributed to Jonathan was actually done by his son. In fact, it was almost immediately after Jonathan's death that the first records of stone removal begin to appear. It would appear that where Jonathan had been a tax collector, Seth was avoiding collection of the quarry tax by using pre-quarried stone from the hilltop. If there was any question as to the difference between the father and the son, it came in 1863, 14 years after Jonathan's death. George Jonathan Pattee, grandson of Jonathan and son of Seth, in 1863, sued his father. It seems that Jonathan's Last Will had been in Seth's possession all along, and that the will left all of the property to George.

By the time that Seth J.M. was forced to probate the will, the hilltop house was gone. Local tradition tells of a fire destroying the house, but there is no archaeological evidence to support this claim – none of the charred wood, charcoal or heat-damaged artifacts indicative of a fire. An Early Sites Foundation excavation in 1955 found only numerous nails. What probably happened was that a fire had damaged the house sometime after Betsy's death in the 1850's? Rather than repair the structure, Seth disassembled the house and barn, salvaged what he could of the brick and wood, and rebuilt at the bottom of the hill on an old colonial tavern foundation. The Seth Mallon Pattee house has been examined; the square footage of the house and attached barn match those from the site, and the age of the wood at cursory glance appears to predate the age of the structure. It is not by any stretch a proven fact, however, it does explain both the persistent fire story and the lack of house structure artifacts.

This reconstruction put the Pattee homestead back on a main road - in the previous decades, the old post road past the base of the hill had been abandoned. This house disassembly also confused later researchers trying to determine how there could be a house on the hill but no remnants of wood and only a minimum of bricks.

Within weeks of George being awarded the property of his grandfather, he sold it to Nathaniel Paul, a local mill owner who proceeded to strip lumber the hill and surrounding properties. Although the property would briefly return once more to the Pattee family (George's sister Anna MacNeil owned the property from 1902-1927), it was the end of an era - the Pattee family had held the property from 1734 to 1863.

When the lumbermen were finished, the site actually looked very similar to its original use. The hill was bare again, offering a spectacular view of the surrounding countryside. So impressive was the view that it became increasingly popular as a picnic locale. Entire school classes held picnics on the hilltop, breaking china, climbing in and out of the ruins, and looking for "Indian" artifacts. By the time the sufficient growth had returned to obscure the view again, the site had been impacted. To this day, shards of china are found. Additional effects of this heavy public traffic include what is now the exit to the oracle chamber. Senior citizens who visit the site today still recall crawling in and out of the oracle chamber looking for arrowheads and skeletons. They remember quite clearly that the township, fearing for children's safety in the stone structures, had sealed the Oracle Chamber. Undaunted, they found and used an alternative entrance. What they were crawling through was a vent that was never designed for supporting the weight of teenage pothunters. As it deteriorated, the hole continued to widen; traffic and weathering removed any chance of reconstruction. Another legacy of these picnickers is a complete lack of surface artifacts - pottery shards, stone tools, even trash from Pattee house, was picked clean.

As the Salem residents frolicked among the strange stone ruins, they wondered about their origins. It was from these casual visitors that the legend of Jonathan Pattee began to grow. Later skeptics were quick to record the various tales that the local residents "remembered". Among the claims made were that Jonathan, being a felon, hid from the sheriff in his caves (hard to do in comparatively shallow structures on a main road in a house full of town poor), that Jonathan and his 5 sons built the site (a neat trick for a man with only one son who lived to adulthood), and that Jonathan was an eccentric who just liked building in stone (Stephen Pattee, Jonathan's brother was a carpenter. Stephen Pattee was mentally unstable and lived on the site for a year with the town poor, but why would a carpenter suddenly switch to building in stone with stone tools, and how did he manage to build a 12 acre site in less than a year?).

The creation of the mythical Jonathan Pattee, an eccentric felon with 5 sons, is that the Pattee family itself has become polarized on the issue of Jonathan's involvement with site construction. The majority of Jonathan's descendants have always maintained that Jonathan never built the site, but that he did "improve" several structures for storage use. But these descendants are rarely quoted and have always been rather laconic about the fuss raised about the whole affair.

Other relatives, widely quoted, are quite vehement about Jonathan's active participation in site construction. Unfortunately, they are also the originators of some of misinformation about their ancestor. If we look at two of them, it illustrates the point more than adequately.

In 1934, the Haverhill Evening Gazette ran an article on the site in which reporter Frank Portors interviewed a local girl about the site. Several days later, the paper ran a follow-up article that featured a rebuttal by Susie Bendel, granddaughter of Seth J.M. Pattee. The trouble is Mrs. Bendel knew very little of her own family, let alone the site's history.

| BENDEL VERSION | ACTUAL DETAIL |
|---|---|
| Great granddaughter of Seth | Great granddaughter of Jona- |

| | |
|---|---|
| Jonathan Pattee who built the site. | than Pattee, Seth Jonathan Mallon Pattee was grandfather |
| Neighbors and others came to help build the caves. It took a long time | No record of such a large undertaking, which would be mentioned in town history. |
| Site used as picnic grove. | Correct, per local residents. |
| Pattees came from France during Revolutionary War (1776). | Pattees arrived in New England in 1676 from England via Virginia. |

This article also marks a clear division among the Pattee family as to the site's origin. The worst story written by a Pattee about Jonathan is a dubious distinction that belongs to Dr. George Woodbury, who also is in the running for possibly penning the nastiest little article of all time. The highlight of this 1958 article is the following conclusion, quoted with grammar errors intact:

> *Jonathan Pattee had a reputation as a local "character" in his time. Legend holds that he settled in this remote spot because of difficulties with the town authorities. There is no doubt he and his five stout sons, lived here that they acquired some local reputation as enthusiastic and eccentric stone masons. The conclusion was they were all "a might touched".*

This portrait is a far cry from the real Jonathan Pattee, the tax collector, litigant, cordwainer, and keeper of the poor who had but one son. Perhaps, based on the persistence of such reoccurring fiction, instead of calling this age the Pattee Age, it might be better to call it the Age of Myth.

The Pattee Family, circa 1905 in front of the house suspected to be rebuilt from Jonathan Pattee's home. Back Row: Susie Pattee Bendel, Susie Pattee McLees, Anna Pattee McNeil, Seth Mallon Pattee. Front Row: Frances McLees, Shirley Bendel. McNeil, McLees and Pattee are Jonathan Pattee's grandchildren. (*Photo from Gilbert's History of Salem, NH, 1907)*

A picnicker poses in front of the East-West Chamber in September of 1920. Such photos are invaluable in determining what condition various structures were in prior to Goodwin's arrival. *(Photo courtesy of George Stackpole)*

# Chapter 6 – The Antiquarian Age

A ntiquarians are a lost breed in this age of specialization, but these dabblers of an earlier age were not only prolific, but successful as well; it was amateur archaeologist Schliemann who found ancient Troy. No subject was too obscure, no phenomena too rare, and most had ample money to fund private collections and publish pet theories. The age of such amateur scholarship arrived late at Mystery Hill, but the impact is still reverberating.

The great American horror writer, H.P. Lovecraft, although never with sufficient resources to qualify as dilettante, was the genteel embodiment of antiquarians, with a passable knowledge of a wide variety of subjects.

H. P. Lovecraft visited Mystery Hill in July of 1928, as chronicled in his most widely read work, "The Dunwich Horror." This famed novelette contains numerous references to legends and locales that Lovecraft had visited in the months prior to writing the tale. Lovecraft scholar Donald Burleson notes that the whippoorwills of Dunwich are from a local legend Lovecraft picked up in Wilbraham, MA. Cold Springs Glen, Burleson also points out, is "faithful in every physical detail" to a ravine visited on one of many trips with fellow fantasy writers H. Warner Munn and Paul Cook in 1928, and that "most of the Dunwich family names in the story are prominent in Athol history - Wheeler, Farr, Sawyer, Bishop."

H. Warner Munn, a fellow writer who accompanied the Providence, RI resident confirmed Lovecraft's visit to the site, but Munn was unable to recall the specific date. It was the last name on the above list, Bishop (or more specifically, Seth Bishop), that gave researchers the initial indication that Lovecraft visited the site in 1928, prior to writing the story. Armitage, Rice, and Morgan, the protagonists of the story, are told of a shortcut to Seth Bishop's house.

*I guess ye kin git to Seth Bishop's quickest by cuttin'*
*acrost the lower medder here, wadin' the brook at the low*

*place an' climbin' through Carrier's mowin' an' the tim-
ber-lot beyont. That comes aout on the upper rud mighty
nigh Seth's - a leetle t'other side.*

This description, as well as the details added in the ensuing
paragraphs, follows very closely the terrain features one would
encounter if one was taking a shortcut cross-country to Mystery Hill from one of the roads surrounding the site, coming out
of the woods on Haverhill Road near Seth Pattee's house.
Looking over the neighborhood, we find a neighbor who is
most assuredly site related - Fred K. Duston.

Fred Duston's 1927 purchase of Pattee land, including Pattee's Caves, made his house a logical location to go if you
wanted to see the caves in 1928. If Duston was to send the
Lovecraft party unescorted from his house to the site along the
wood trails ringing the hill, the directions would parallel the
above quoted directions; from Fred Duston's farmhouse in his
lower meadow, cross a small brook into the meadows previously owned by Dudley Currier, heading onto Taylor land, and
then into Parker's woodlot. This brings you out on Haverhill
road near the Seth Pattee house. Across from the Pattee house
was the dirt road that led to the summit. If the Lovecraft entou-
rage, unfamiliar with the path, had veered off onto a lumber
road which forks off northerly from the main trail (Armitage's
group was stopped in the story as they started to wander), they
would have encountered the glacial cliffs west of the site, the
perpendicular wooded hill referred to in the story.

Arriving at the site, Lovecraft saw the stone ruins atop the
hill, seemingly centered on the 4 1/2-ton sacrificial table. Fred
Duston would have been well versed in local lore on Pattee's
caves, including the rumors of skeletal remains being found
about the site. It is no great stretch of the imagination to trans-
form Mystery Hill's stone ruins and legends into the skull-
strewn altar atop Sentinel Hill.

It is not surprising that Lovecraft interprets the site as an altar site, although it is one of the few that refer to it as a nexus
of evil forces. The only other possible site affiliation with the

powers of darkness is a persistent rumor of a visit to Mystery Hill by the infamous Aleister Crowley. This story has persisted for some time, with published reports of the theory as recently as 1983. Site detractors use this visit by Crowley as a theory of last resort, to suggest the source of the various inscriptions found in the vicinity are from recent, rather than ancient, pagan ceremonies.

Crowley visited the United States on three separate occasions, including a five-year stay starting in 1914. It is during that extended visit of 1914-1919 that Crowley began to take infrequent trips to Lake Pasquaney in New Hampshire for "magical retirements." Various stories recounted by Crowley and his biographers of these trips include encounters with ball lightning, sacrificial ceremonies involving frogs, and what is referred to as the "star sponge vision."

Aleister Crowley is not noted for a succinct writing style, as evidenced by numerous interpretations of his texts. Crowley assigns archaic or arcane aliases to locations and persons discussed in his texts. The location of Lake Pasquaney is of a similar nature - there is no lake bearing that name in New Hampshire. Various texts discussing Crowley's New Hampshire retreats either gloss over the specific location or arbitrarily assign the name to a contemporary lake. Because the specific location of Lake Pasquaney is necessary for determining Crowley's proximity to America's Stonehenge while in New Hampshire, it becomes vital to identify the location. The only clue comes from Crowley's diary entry of 23 June 1916, which places him in Bristol, New Hampshire. This puts him squarely in the New Hampshire Lakes region, but still does not identify which lake is the one in question.

It is ironic that an author whose surname is well known at America's Stonehenge - Pattee, identifies Lake Pasquaney. In the same time period that Jonathan Pattee resided on Mystery Hill, Fred Lewis Pattee was beginning his extensive career in American literature. This distantly related Pattee was noted for his textbooks on American literature, but he also published less scholarly volumes of poetry and rustic musings. One such book was among his earliest; a remembrance of the lake near his Alexandria, New Hampshire home entitled Lake Pasquaney. In the preface, Pattee remarks on his use of Pasquaney rather than "the more orthodox Newfound." The 1893 publication date of Pattee's book suggests that the name Newfound Lake had already replaced Lake Pasquaney 25 years before Crowley's visit.

The possibility of Aleister Crowley visiting Mystery Hill suddenly becomes extremely remote. The closest Crowley could have come to the site is a train bound from Lowell, MA to Nashua, NH enroute to Newfound Lake.

This does not end the theory of contemporary pagan cults being responsible for the various inscriptions found on Mystery Hill.

However, it may remove the notorious Aleister Crowley from the theory, hopefully taking most of the persistence and vitality of the claim with him.

Another antiquarian laying claim to Mystery Hill is Ohio State University Professor Wilbur H. Siebert, an acknowledged expert in the study of the Underground Railroad. This legendary secret network spirited escaped slaves out of the slave states to freedom. Between 1830 and 1860, as many as 100,000 fugitives may have fled to Canada, following the invisible trail from house to house, church to barn. In 1898, at the height of the antiquarian craze in the country, Siebert authored *Underground Railroad from Slavery to Freedom*, published while participants were still alive to contribute their recollections. Because of this book, various people and groups, all anxious to have their local Underground Railroad stop documented by Professor Siebert, contacted him. This was also part of the antiquarian phenomena - local historical societies were founded everywhere, and the societies then published town histories. Underground Railroad stories were as vital a part of these histories as were the tales of brave colonists fighting off those bloodthirsty Indians. Siebert began compiling these new correspondences into articles and books. Mystery Hill is included in a path leading north from Andover to Lawrence, Massachusetts. The stop in question was the house of Mr. Joseph W. Poor:

> *When Mr. Poor heard a gentle rap on his door or other subdued sound in the night, he dressed quickly, went out, harnessed his mare Nellie into a covered wagon and started with his dusky passengers, probably for North Salem, New Hampshire. On the top of a hill at that place were several large excavations, lined and covered with slabs of stone, which had furnished retreats for the neighboring inhabitants when the Indians were on the warpath, but which now afforded refuge to fugitive slaves. Mr. Poor was always home for breakfast.*

There are several problems with this account, not the least of which is the time frame. Jonathan Pattee lived on the site until his death in 1849, and his son was probably there another 2 years. During the time Jonathan was there, he had the town paupers on the property. It would not be likely that a secret network would send fugitives to a location with an active house on it. Even if Jonathan was an abolitionist, the risk of discovery would be too great with a dozen paupers in the house. However, after 1852, with Jonathan dead and Seth Jonathan Mallon moved into his new house, the property would indeed be ideal for an Underground Railroad stopover. The house may or may not have been standing after 1852, but the chambers were there for hiding, and the abandoned post road could be used as a northerly path.

The primary problem with the designation as an Underground Railroad stop is Professor Siebert's source material. Siebert's materials on the Underground Railroad, housed at the Ohio Historical Society, indicates his source for the Mystery Hill designation was correspondence with Miss Marion LeMere of Andover, Massachusetts. LeMere's source was the 1934 Haverhill Evening Gazette article. This article features an interview with a local teenager, Elsie Conley. This article also has several errors, primarily names and time periods, but there are also several facts that were proved correct at much later dates. A quick comparison demonstrates the point.

| CONLEY VERSION | ACTUAL DETAIL |
|---|---|
| No mention of site in town records. | Correct – however, extant town records from the time period are scarce. |
| Record book of Samuel J. Pattee mentions cave on property. Pattee died 60 years prior (c.1860) | No Samuel J. Pattee in family genealogical records. Possible reference to Seth J. Pattee with Jonathan's death date. Record book may be reference to Gilbert's History. |
| Large flat rock on ground used for winepress, With furrow for drain. | Sacrificial table prior to Goodwin appeared as if on surface. Winepress claim is a persistent one. |
| Old Indian trail, later post road ran near hill. | Confirmed in the late 1980's. Extant part is now bridle path called Pope Road. |

As a sidebar, the Susie Bendel article mention previously appears as a rebuttal to the Conley interview several days later.

It is highly unlikely that the Underground Railroad question will ever be resolved fully. Since aiding escaped slaves was a federal offense, there were no records kept which could prove or disprove such a claim. However, as stated above, the site would be an ideal location after 1852 - isolated structures in the woods, near an abandoned road. Seth Jonathan Mallon Pattee may have indeed been the next stop on the Underground Railroad, using the ruins on the hill above his house. He was active in the local Methodist church, and his son, Seth Mallon, was also involved in civic affairs. The case for hiding fugitive slaves on the site is based strictly in local tradition and circumstantial evidence, but so are the claims of every other stop on the great trail northward to freedom. Without any evidence to contradict the stories, Mystery Hill's claim as an contradict the stories, Mystery Hill's claim as an Underground Railroad stop is as valid as any other.

In the summer of 1936, the most significant antiquarian arrived at the site. Called both a savior and a sinner, his presence continues to be felt on Mystery Hill - William B. Goodwin.

> *From that day when we [first] ... gazed in perplexity at the jumble of rocks on the Site at North Salem, we could not help but realize that these were no ordinary or haphazard remains of man's handiwork but the living, if silent, proof of a long forgotten past. Well do we remember our astonishment. Instinctively we had to stop and sit down on the stone by the tall pine in the plaza, covering our face with our hands to shut in the picture of desolation around us, trying to think out what this utterly un-American set-up might mean.*

Goodwin first visited the site in July of 1936, and by April of 1937, had purchased the property. In a letter written soon after that first trip he wrote:

> *I have just been to visit the most amazing ruins of a stone village in New Hampshire that I have ever seen anywhere... I am wondering if I have found the village site of the lost Norwegian Colony in Western Greenland that we know came from there in 1344 and amalgamated with the Indians, or as the papal records say "went native". I can't begin to describe it; I haven't the time in the first place; it is the most amazing thing I have ever seen.*

William Goodwin's fascination with his North Salem village would overshadow a successful career both in business and in antiquarian pursuits. An avid collector, his interests ranged from antique maps to colonial chests. However Goodwin was not content with just collecting, he researched the fields he collected in. Not content with merely owning the colonial chests, he began researching the identities of colonial furniture makers, becoming an expert in the identities of early Massachusetts cabinetmakers. As he became further and further immersed in this hobby, he began an acquaintance with Wallace Nutting, a well-known colonial furniture collector and furniture restorer. When Nutting was preparing to sell his vast collection of furniture, it was William Goodwin who acted as go between, convincing Nutting to sell to the Wadsworth Athenaeum in Hartford, CT (Goodwin, his brother and his father all were actively involved with this museum), rather than any of the larger museum clamoring for it. The crowning achievement to this acquisition was when Goodwin convinced his cousin J.P. Morgan to underwrite the purchase. Goodwin, who expected (and received) no acknowledgment of these backstage manipulations, would be appointed to the honorary position of "Curator of Colonial Arts." He would cherish this title the rest of his life, buying colonial houses and stripping all paneling and metalwork out for the Athenaeum, then refurbishing the property for rentals. To this day, the Nutting Collection in Hartford is considered the foremost collection of colonial furniture extant.

William Brownell Goodwin was born October 07, 1866, the second child of Reverend Francis and Mary (Jackson) Goodwin. He was an 8th generation direct descendant of Ozias Goodwin, a founder of Hartford. He was named for his uncle, Dr. William R. Brownell, a decorated Civil War surgeon and Hartford physician whose wife, Sarah Morgan Goodwin Brownell, was Francis Goodwin's only sister. Sarah Brownell had died 8 months before William's birth, just 3 days after her first wedding anniversary. All in all, Will Goodwin was born into the American equivalent of a blueblood family- comfortably wealthy (with old money), socially elite and civic minded. Will Goodwin, however, was born with a restless streak.

He attended St. Paul's School in Concord, New Hampshire, a private Episcopalian high school. When he started at Trinity College, it appeared as though Will would follow in the path of his father and older brother James - a theological degree and a life of public service. Will Goodwin had other ideas. After a year at Trinity, he transferred to Yale University but found little to keep his attention. The exception was athletics. As a member of Yale's 1886 & 1887 track teams, he held the University records for both high jump and broad jump.

Also while at Yale, he attended a lecture by Hartford resident Samuel Clemens. Whether hearing of Mark Twain's travels was the catalyst or not, Will's restless spirit finally prevailed. He learned of a position as a bank clerk in Kansas City and immediately headed west. After 2 years along the Missouri River, he continued westward in search of adventure. 1889 found Will Goodwin in Seattle, climbing the ladder of success. His restlessness drove him; he became a Director for Mechanics Mill and Lumber Company, and then a partner in a wholesale pork-packing firm. His love of athletics came with him to the growing city. In 1889, he organized the first college football team (American Rugby rules) on the Pacific Coast at the University of Washington. The next year, he arranged the first international boat race on the West Coast, between Vancouver and Seattle. In 1892, he founded the Seattle Athletic Club.

By 1895, Aetna Fire Insurance Company was expanding their operations into the rapidly growing city. Goodwin, with his knowledge of the city, his business background, and his Hartford family connections, was hired as special agent for Actna Insurance Company of Hartford.

Then in 1898, the word came back from the wilderness gold. Goodwin heeded the call and set forth into the wilderness and into the Yukon Gold Rush. NorthWest Mounted Police records for Jun 9, 1898 noted that among the hundreds of crossings into the Yukon was W.B. Goodwin of Seattle. Will Goodwin spent two years prospecting for gold.

Although he did not strike it rich, it was a learning experience. He passingly mentioned the trip from Seattle into Canadian wilderness above the Arctic Circle, but in his four books, he dropped many hints of the experiences of those days: navigating the Yukon River in an overloaded canoe, living among the Indians, delivering supplies to the prospectors. After two summers of swamps filled with mosquitoes and black flies and two winters on the Arctic Circle, Goodwin returned to Seattle. Although he would appear robust the rest of his life, he would find it progressively more difficult to cope with the cold

In the fall of 1899, he returned from the Yukon gold fields. So smoothly had Aetna's operations continued even in his absence that Aetna offered him a new challenge - San Francisco. He agreed, but only after marrying Mary A. Hood of Seattle on November 23, 1899.

San Francisco in 1899 was a growing city. Shipping and railroads continued the growth started fifty years past by the original Comstock gold rush. Now San Francisco's only gold related industry was as port of arrival and tack supplier for the East Coast optimists enroute to the Yukon.

As a Special Agent, Goodwin's primary function was to verify the value of insured buildings and risks to that building, adjusting the insurance accordingly. This left him with time to visit the libraries and museums of the area. On one such jaunt in December of 1899, Will Goodwin ran across an acquaintance from his days in the Yukon - Fred Berry. Berry was in a quandary. He was finalizing a football game and needed impartial, competent officials after disastrous officiating at the Thanksgiving game. Will's background in athletics made him a natural choice. This added another interesting footnote to his career: Referee of the very first transcontinental championship football game.

The game was between the Carlisle Pennsylvania Indian School and the varsity team of University of California at Berkeley. However, the game was planned on very short notice, and several of the Berkeley players were not longer in the area. Ringers were brought in from the Stanford Team, the first of several controversies. Sand on the playing field gave the California team the edge (since the Indians only played on turf), then California insisted on a larger, non-regulation football. Goodwin conceded these points to the California team although it gave them the advantage, then watched as the Carlisle Indians still won 2-0. It was the beginning and the end of Goodwin's career in officiating, but he was so impressed by the Carlisle Indians that when he wrote *Ruins of Great Ireland in New England* 45 years later, he still clearly remembered the episode.

By 1901, Goodwin had moved from officiating to coaching, first training the University of California's crew and then the Olympic Club's in 1902. In 1903, he brought about the first intercollegiate race on the Pacific Coast, a four-oared race at Seattle between University of California and his former associates at the University of Seattle.

In 1904, Goodwin accepted a promotion to special agent for Ohio and West Virginia and was transferred to Columbus, Ohio. Again, his timing proved fortuitous, for less than two years later, on Apr. 18, 1906, San Francisco suffered a major earthquake; the resulting 3-day fire razed the core of the city. Apparently, Aetna's claims from this calamity were not excessive - Will Goodwin knew his insurance, and Aetna made note of it; in 1908, he was appointed State Agent for Ohio. With this promotion came vast amounts of travel, which Goodwin used to his advantage. He began collaboration with the State Highway Department, mapping the various routes to the assorted mound sites in the state. It was not archaeology but it was close. He would go into an area, learn of small, unknown mound sites, write up directions to them, and pass the information on. He also learned on his travels that Ohio was an antique collector's paradise. He acquired a colonial chest, which gave birth to a new love of collecting. His zealous pursuit of the origins of his acquisitions was the start of his long correspondence with Wallace Nutting, considered the foremost collector of the time.

By 1915, the strain of the workload began to tax Will's health, especially when winter snows would affect his vitality. On the verge of collapse, he was ordered by his physician to spend the winter in a warmer climate. He and Mary decided on Jamaica. So impressed with the island nation were the Goodwins that they returned to Jamaica every year until 1937, when World War II forced cancellation of the tradition.

Even on vacation, Will Goodwin's restless spirit drove him on. Each trip he explored more of the Jamaica. Soon, he discovered that he knew the location of more Spanish sites on the island than the local British authorities. Within a few years, he was able to tell English from Spanish ruins at a glimpse.

Meanwhile, back in Ohio, Goodwin was developing a reputation as a canny antique collector. His correspondence with Wallace Nutting, and his father, as past president of the Wadsworth Athenaeum, assured him of contacts needed to actively pursue choice pieces. His preference was for cabinets, plain or carved, from the colonial era, but he also took a liking to old maps.

Things started changing quickly in the 1920's. Wallace Nutting began publishing a series of books on early American furniture including photographs of pieces owned by William Goodwin. Not only did this enhance his status as a collector, but it also increased the number of opportunities to purchase additional pieces.

Wallace relates a story that shows the measure of William Goodwin more than other source. It seems that two elderly ladies found their income was becoming insufficient to support them. To supplement their resources, they began selling off family heirlooms. However, their most valuable pieces of antique furniture were bought by an unscrupulous dealer at a fraction of the worth. Goodwin, when apprised of the situation, attempted to remedy the situation, only to find the transaction, although unfair, was completely legal. Goodwin, on a subsequent visit with the elderly sisters, was offered the last household items left to sell - a trunk of old papers. Goodwin, although not interested in the item, offered them an amount above the value. Taking the chest home, he found his initial assessment was correct - the chest contained letters, deeds, and various documents of limited interest and less value. At the bottom of the chest however, he found a sheet with a wax seal. Suspecting this might have some value, he took this for appraisal by an expert. Upon examination, it was discovered to be a business transaction containing the signature of Button Gwinnett, the rarest autograph of all the signers of the Declaration of Independence. Goodwin immediately sent the document out to auction, and raised sixteen thousand dollars. Although the legal owner, Goodwin turned the full amount over to the elderly women. Of such a caliber of gentleman was Goodwin that he asked for no recognition. In fact, at his insistence, the story was soon modified to "an anonymous collector."

In 1924, William Goodwin was promoted again, this time to the home office. Thirty-three years after he left, Goodwin returned to Hartford, moving into his father's house. His brother Charles, now a prominent attorney in Hartford, was appointed to the Board of Directors of Aetna, alongside Cousin J.P. Morgan. Suddenly, he found himself on the fast track. In 1926, he was appointed an officer of Aetna's World Fire & Marine Insurance Company.

In 1927, he was elected to the Walpole Society, an extremely exclusive group of antique collectors whose ranks included such noted collectors as Henry Francis du Pont, whose collection would become Winterthur Museum. But even as he joined the ranks of collecting elite, his interests began to go beyond merely acquisition. Part of Goodwin's expertise came from his willingness to invest hours into research - poring over old maps and books, tracking back sources, and verifying material. Now, his explorations in Jamaica were proving to him that fieldwork could be just as invigorating. William Goodwin began field excavations.

In 1931, William B. Goodwin retired from the Insurance business. At the time, he was an officer of two Aetna subsidiaries, World Fire and Marine Insurance, and Century Indemnity. He was active in the Walpole Society, the Wadsworth Athenaeum, the Hartford Club, and the Society of Descendants of the Founders of Hartford. He was also supervising seasonal excavations in Rhode Island and Jamaica. William Goodwin's retirement made his workload even heavier.

The Rhode Island Historical published Goodwin's "Notes Regarding Origin of Fort Ninigret" in January of 1932. In this, one of his earliest articles, he showed the style of writing that all his works exhibited: extensive support documentation from historical text, summaries of excavation results, and little detail on actual fieldwork.

In 1935, he purchased an ancient ax head found in Nova Scotia that he believed to be Norse in origin. Goodwin wrote to an old acquaintance from his Washington days, runic expert Olaf Strandwold on this topic.

This was a catalyst that took Will Goodwin in a new direction.

Strandwold was preparing a book for publication, and had sent a number of inquiries to newspapers in New England, trying to track down the lost locations of reported inscribed stones. One such inquiry was in the *Boston Globe,* regarding a stone in Hampton, NH that Strandwold had learned of from a 1902 Philadelphia newspaper article. He eventually learned the location of the stone, known locally as 'Thorvald's Rock." Both Goodwin's axe and the Hampton site would be included in Strandwold's *Norse Runic Inscriptions along the Atlantic Seaboard.*

Of far more importance to the site in North Salem, it brought Strandwold's work to the attention of a young man with a mysterious "cave" on his family property in Upton, Massachusetts. This correspondent was named Malcolm Pearson.

Malcolm Pearson was, and still is, a photographer. His photographs of runestones, lithic structures and carvings fill the books of Strandwold, Goodwin and a myriad of other authors. His earliest contact with New England's lithic ruins was when his parents bought that house in Upton, MA with a stone structure in woods behind it. Pearson was determined to learn the origins of this structure, now known as the Upton Beehive. As Pearson and Strandwold continued corresponding, Strandwold asked Goodwin to investigate Pearson's mysterious structure on his behalf. A letter directly from Goodwin to Pearson began a collaboration that not lasted the rest of Goodwin's life, but beyond. To this day, the work of Pearson and Goodwin are inseparable. In fact, it was Malcolm Pearson who first brought the North Salem site to the attention of William Goodwin.

When Goodwin arrived in Upton, Malcolm showed him the structure, and mentioned a village of stone ruins in North Salem he had recently visited after learning of them in an October 1935 *Boston Globe* article. Three weeks later, Pearson and Goodwin headed into New Hampshire to visit the stone ruins that later became known as Mystery Hill. Goodwin immediately had Pearson track down the owner and by April, William Goodwin owned the stone village free and clear.

Goodwin ostensibly bought the site as part of his research into the location of Vinland. However, it took very little time to convince him of his error. Leaving Vinland at Portsmouth, NH where his book *Truth About Leif Ericsson* placed it, he decided instead that this must be Hvitramannaland - Great Ireland of the Norse sagas. Goodwin then launched a full-fledged investigation, drawing together a vast amount of obscure information about the Culdee Monks whose monastery he believed he now owned. Goodwin's theory was that the Culdees, rather than resist Nordic interference, merely abandoned their settlements as the Norse neared, being driven westward from Ireland to Iceland to Greenland. At this point, the Culdees disappeared and were assumed to have returned to Ireland and assimilated into the mainstream Roman Catholic Church. Goodwin argued that a few of the Culdees continued westward and settled in North America. His argument was built on circumstantial evidence: beehive huts along Indian trails far from the shore, and oral traditions from Icelandic sagas. These were proposed as proof that the Culdees had set up a vast project to convert the Algonquins to Christianity, dwelling near the pagan Native Americans but always far enough inland to avoid the marauding Norse.

The only thing missing was artifact evidence. To this end, Goodwin had Pearson assemble a team of workmen and build a 4-bunk cabin on the hilltop. Pearson then orchestrated a fence around the site (which still stands) and went to work. Although his books would suggest otherwise, Goodwin spent very little time at his stone village.

Instead he left the site under the supervision of Malcolm Pearson. Pearson would write to Goodwin, Goodwin would answer, and work progressed. Prior to World War II, Goodwin would have his chauffeur drive him up to oversee the work. After the war broke out, with the accompanying gas restrictions, Goodwin would take the train from Hartford to Worcester, MA where Pearson would pick him up. Pearson, as a media photojournalist, received additional gasoline rations, which allowed him to take Goodwin to the site, stopping to investigate other sites along the way.

Even by 1930's standards, Goodwin's excavation directives left much to be desired. When he suspected that the sacrificial table might not be resting on the surface, Goodwin had the area cleared of soil build-up to expose that the table sat on stone legs in a recess that had filled completely with soil. Consequently, current researchers have no way of knowing whether or not the table is supposed to be on exposed legs or if the legs are merely a frame to hold the table steady while soil was placed around it. A simple soil profile would clear that up immediately, but there is none.

The sacrificial table prior to Goodwin's excavations *(Malcolm Pearson photo)*

By this time, there was a new figure developing a reputation within historical circles - Samuel Eliot Morison of Harvard University. Morison was similar to Goodwin in many ways. Both were direct, opinionated, confident of their research and very sensitive to criticism. It was inevitable the two would clash.

In 1937, Morison began the first of four trips in sailing vessels, attempting to approximate the voyages of Columbus, the same year Goodwin purchased the Mystery Hill site. Within a year, the "Irish Monastery" was receiving national coverage, thanks to a writer named Clay Perry. Perry had resigned from the WPA to write a book on New England caves. He had been running letters to the editors in as many newspapers that would print them, in search of local caves. Goodwin, as owner of a "manmade cave" (the oracle chamber) dropped him a note. Perry took it from there, using the site to get himself published in magazines and newspapers across the country. Goodwin himself only participated in one article, a Sunday supplement piece in the Hartford Courant. The number of visitors and encouragement that he received inspired him. In 1938, Goodwin submitted a brief history of the "stone village site" to the *New England Quarterly*, the editorial board of which included Samuel Eliot Morison.

Goodwin was at this time several years into excavations at Don Christopher's Cove in St. Ann's Bay off Jamaica. Goodwin's expressed desire was to find the remains of Columbus' last two ships, ditched in that cove during his last, ill-fated voyage. Morison visited the excavation site while Goodwin was away, but the two exchanged correspondences about the location.

Morison had already established a very specific stance on the subject of any and all European explorations prior to Columbus. The stance is today referred to as NEBC, or No Explorers Before Columbus. Although later academians take the expression literally, Morison meant it figuratively; Regardless whether another European culture had reached the New World, colonized, explored it and/or exploited it, the impact on the New World was ephemeral and long forgotten. Hence any explorations before Columbus were inconsequential. Goodwin's theory about an Irish Monastery in New Hampshire was therefore irrelevant to Morison. Additionally, Morison was finishing preparations for publication of his first major book on Columbus, *The Second Voyage of Christopher Columbus From Cadiz to Hispanolia.* Morison, instead of using Goodwin's article, sent a colleague to North Salem to write a new article. Hugh O'Neill Hencken was the curator of European Archeology at Harvard's Peabody Museum. Hencken visited the site several times. He reviewed Goodwin's material and then wrote a very polite and very thorough article completely discrediting the Irish Monastery theory.

"The 'Irish Monastery' At North Salem, New Hampshire" ran in the September 1939 issue of *New England Quarterly.* Hencken's article focused on two specific issues. The first was whether or not the site was indeed a medieval Irish construction. Goodwin's use of early Icelandic sagas to establish the existence of a North American Irish presence was examined. Goodwin primarily used four passages, one from the *Landnamabok,* one from Manuscript AM 770 (which appears to be a retelling of the *Landnamabok*) a reference from the *Eyrbyggja Saga*, and a portion of the visit of Thorfinn Karlsefni to North America. A good example of how the article went is Hencken's assessment of the use of *Landnamabok*, which Hencken refers to as "an ancient and on the whole reliable text," except for the section utilized by Goodwin, which was "not on par with the rest." Hencken then demonstrates that the Pattee's Cave site had no characteristics in common with monastery sites in Ireland except for use of corbelled vaulting in the roof of the Y-Chamber, which was not conclusive, since corbelling appears across the globe.

Interestingly enough, Hencken mentions that Goodwin has overlooked the similarity of the Y-Chamber to the early Irish structure known as a souterrain, although souterrains were lower inside.

The second issue then to be addressed, having eliminated the Culdees, was who constructed the site. Hencken makes note of several features on the site that predate Jonathan Pattee, including a white pine stump whose roots had grown into the stone wall of a structure well before Jonathan's birth but concludes that the local tradition that Jonathan Pattee, being an eccentric, probably constructed the bulk of the site with his large family and teams of oxen. A footnote on the final page of the article thanks Dr. George Woodbury for his assistance, so the "Jonathan was an eccentric" theory came from within the family again.

Malcolm Pearson recalls one visit to the site where he and Goodwin had stood on the ramp leading to the sacrificial table with Hencken, and Hencken commented on the similarity of the stonework to that he had seen on the British Isles. Needless to say, when the article came out, Goodwin was bitterly disappointed. He blamed Hencken, not Morison. This however was about to change.

In 1940, Morison published an article on the location of Columbus' colonization attempt at La Navidad. That same year, Goodwin published the results of his 1935-38 unsuccessful excavations as *The Lure of Gold*. In this book, he mentions his opinion that he thought Morison's location of La Navidad was incorrect. Morison immediately ran an abridged version of Hencken's work in *Scientific American*. This abridged version is considerable shorter, considerably harsher, and infers that documentation is available in the longer *New England Quarterly* article. It isn't there, but in that time period, access to the regional, smaller circulation magazine was more difficult, and most readers would have to take the article on faith. Although several more articles would run featuring the Irish monk theory, Morison had effectively removed Goodwin's credibility, and Goodwin's Irish Monastery quickly lost the interest of the media.

As Goodwin's stature and health began to decline, Morison's reputation climbed. In 1941, Goodwin submitted an article to a new scholarly journal on maritime studies, *American*

*Neptune,* suggesting that Norse crossings on the Atlantic were done in merchant trading ships, not dragon ships (a view that would prove correct). Goodwin was unaware that Morison was a founder and editor of this journal, at least until the article was unconditionally rejected. Goodwin took the article, added his voluminous historical notes, and produced his second book, *The Truth about Leif Ericsson.*

The next year, Morison published *Admiral in the Ocean Sea*, a Pulitzer Prize winning biography of Columbus. This book established Morison as the country's foremost historian; the book carefully omits any reference to Goodwin's excavations at Don Christopher's Cove.

Goodwin was painfully aware of the snub, but continued to underwrite excavations at North Salem during the summers. His health was still deteriorating, and his actual visits to the site were becoming fewer with each season, and the burden of supervision fell to Pearson. Goodwin continued working but his research no longer took him far from Hartford.

In 1944, the 81-year-old Goodwin read an address on the history of Saybrook, Connecticut before the Society of the Descendants of the Founders of Hartford. It was well received, and published in pamphlet form. Encouraged by this small triumph, he began assembling his notes on the North Salem site and his remaining material on Jamaica into book form.

In 1945, Goodwin visited the site only long enough to meet with archaeologist Junius Bird. Bird, on his way to a site in Labrador, Canada took time to conduct a week of excavations. When Bird left for Canada, he was convinced the site was not colonial. His basic conclusion was that he didn't know what it was, but that it merited further research. This was small consolation to Goodwin, but at least a professional archaeologist had refuted Hencken's Pattee conclusion.

In 1946, Goodwin's final two books were published. *Spanish and English Ruins in Jamaica* was a follow up to *Lure of Gold,* focusing on Don Diego Columbus's 1509 plan to build a city in Jamaica. There had been sufficient time to prepare this material for publication, but not so *The Ruins of Great Ireland in New England.*

Even a cursory glance through *Ruins* shows the haste with which the material was prepared for publication. There is no fluidity to the prose; packets of Goodwin's notes were simply typeset onto the page. Consequently, material is rehashed in completely different sections of the book, and pages from other published works are added to the jumble without citation. Goodwin also finally broke the silence on his opinions about Morison, who he simply refers to as "Young Columbus," launching into a lengthy diatribe about petty scholars, thwarted funding, blocked articles, and general boorish behavior.

The book was rushed not only because Goodwin's failing health demanded it, but also because, in that age of war induced paper shortages, Malcolm Pearson had been able to locate a supply of book quality paper and there was no way to tell when another such supply would be available. To this day, Malcolm Pearson still clearly remembers hauling the paper from Commonwealth Press in Worcester to the publisher in Boston in the back of the 1938 Chevrolet Station Wagon for which Goodwin allowed him unlimited use.

On May 17, 1950, William Brownell Goodwin died in Hot Springs, Virginia.

After his death, Goodwin became academia's personal whipping boy, being blamed for everything from incompetence to building the site with a team of oxen. Morison's colleagues never recognized Morison's stance as a personal feud, and Goodwin (and Pattee) became progressively more and more the easy answer to the stone ruins in New Hampshire.

So deep did this animosity run that fifteen years after Goodwin's death, Morison, in his *European Discovery of America (Northern Voyages),* was still taking cheap shots at his rival. Morison now admitted to the possibility of Irish in North America, citing the same references in the Vinland Sagas as did Goodwin. This places Hencken's refutation in a difficult position, since his primary argument was the unreliability of the sagas - not the sagas as a whole, merely certain passages -

those quoted by Goodwin. In fact, Morison and Goodwin's major point of contention turns out not to be whether or not Culdees came to America, but whether Mystery Hill was an Culdee site.

Morison died in 1976. Within ten years of his death, his influence on Columbus and his journeys had been reduced to that of a handful of prior researchers – borderline anonymity. In November 1987, National Geographic Magazine ran an article of the search for La Navidad. Goodwin had been correct about Morison's location of the colony being in error. In November of 1986, National Geographic officially located Columbus' first landing site on Samana Cay, some 60 nautical miles away from Morison's Watling Island and then backs it up with cartographic, historical, geographic, and archaeological evidence.

In his will, Goodwin left the North Salem site to his protégé and partner, Malcolm Pearson. Pearson simply did not have the resources to continue the search for answers, and although occasional excavations would take place, the site fell into disuse.

When William Goodwin's obituary ran in the New York Times, it referred to him as a "noted archeologist." Not once in all of his writings or correspondence did he ever refer to himself as an archaeologist. He considered himself a dabbler, an amateur historian, and a scholar. In other words, he was an antiquarian. And in this age of increasingly fine lines of specialization, he may have been the last of a lost breed.

William B. Goodwin during a 1940 research trip on the Piscataqua River near Portsmouth, NH, in preparation for the publication of *The Truth About Leif Ericsson*. *(Malcolm Pearson photo)*

# Chapter 7 – The Stone Age

The current age at America's Stonehenge began in 1955 when an electronic engineer ignored a "no trespassing" sign and by doing so, changed the face of North American archaeology. Subsequent owner Malcolm Pearson had erected the sign in question on Goodwin's fence. The engineer in question was named, most appropriately, Robert Stone.

In the summer of 1955, Bob Stone was sitting in a Derry, NH barbershop, waiting his turn. He happened to thumb through an old *New Hampshire Profiles* magazine and ran across an article about "The North Salem Mystery." Stone had previously heard about the "Pattee's Caves" on a radio program, "Yankee Yarns," out of Boston, but after reading this August 1952 article with photographs of the strange stone constructs, he simply had to see it himself. The barber let Stone have the three year-old magazine, and Bob showed the text to his wife Dot and his brother and sister-in-law, Irv and Kay Dicey. It turned out that Irv knew the site well, and he and Kay had been there many times on picnics. The next day, Bob, Dot, Kay and Irv drove to North Salem, parked on the street and walked up an old dirt path to the site. The dirt path, now usually referred to as Goodwin Road, had been Goodwin's main access from the paved road to his one-acre lot on the summit, but it had originally been a route from Jonathan Pattee's house to Seth Jonathan Mallon Pattee's. It was probably created to move the disassembled house and barn to its new location.

Goodwin's fence still encompasses the main site, but in 1955, it barely slowed down visitors who simply slipped beneath it at any one of a number of erosion gaps between fence and ground level. Bob Stone followed suit and, while his party waited outside the fence; he wandered about the site in disbelief. When he finally crawled back out, his wife asked him what he thought of the place. Robert Stone looked solemnly at the three of them and announced that some day, he would own the entire thing. Bob no longer remembers Dot's exact re-

Malcolm Pearson in 1955. His inheritance of the site 5 years prior would usher in a new age of research when he allowed Bob Stone to lease the property. *(Photo courtesy of Malcoln*

sponse, but he distinctly recalls a comparison between those rocks on the site and those in his head.

By the end of that summer, Stone had contacted Malcolm Pearson as to the possibility of buying or leasing the site; only to learn that Pearson had already leased the property to a research organization he had helped found, "Early Sites Foundation." Early Sites was conducting archaeological work on the property, having contracted with archaeologist Gary Vescelius to investigate the site.

Actually, by the time Bob Stone contacted Malcolm Pearson that summer, Vescelius and his three-man team had already completed their six-week series of excavations. Vescelius had been an assistant to archaeologist Junius Bird in the 1945 excavation for William Goodwin.

Bird was fascinated by the site back in 1945, but could find no evidence to support Goodwin's claims of a European culture. Now, a decade later, as a founder of the Early Sites Foundation, he mapped out a new plan for Vescelius.

Vescelius' only published report was three paragraphs long in Eastern States Archeological Federation's *Bulletin*. His unpublished report to Early Sites is 60 pages long, the majority of which is a one-line inventory of artifacts found. His conclusion was that the site was less than 200 years old. Bird, however, remained unconvinced, as did others in Early Sites. There are numerous problems with the report, not the least of which was Vescelius' use of the mythological version of Jonathan Pattee. In fact, Vescelius takes the Pattee legend to new heights:

> *Though in respects the Caves resemble certain Old World megalithic ruins, the similarities are not in themselves great enough to warrant belief in an historical relationship... It is, perhaps, worth noting in this connection that the Pattees are said to have come from Brittany, and that at least one branch of the family resided for a time on the Isle of Jersey, in the English Channel. Megalithic ruins abound, of course, both in Brittany and on the Channel Isles, and it is conceivable that the eccentric Jonathan embarked upon his cave-building venture under the influence of some tale about huge stone monuments - a tale passed on from one generation of Pattees to the next.*

Even Hencken's dissection of Goodwin's theory doesn't take the Pattee legend to this extreme. The genealogy of the Pattee family has been discussed in a previous chapter, and it seems most likely that Vescelius' research into the Pattee genealogy consisted only of reading Ezra Stearn's *Genealogical and Family History of the State of New Hampshire.* Stearn's history of the state not only borrows heavily from the earlier Pattee profile in Harriman's history of Warner, NH, but also combines it with the French Huguenot Pettee family (whose ancestry was from the Isle of Jersey).

Vescelius's report states that he found more than 8,000 artifacts, all of which he identified as colonial or post-colonial. Therefore, in a time period of six weeks, Vescelius and three assistants found, sorted and examined 8,000 items. Additionally, his excavations took place within the one-acre area that was known to have had a colonial/post-colonial occupation (Pattee) and prior excavations (Goodwin). At least two of his excavations took place in the immediate area that was known to have had the Pattee house on it.

Professional archaeologists, those who refuse to consider the possibility of the site being ancient, assail the validity of the site by noting that the only professional who excavated on the hill had concluded it was colonial. They fail to recall that Junius B. Bird, whose obituary in *American Anthropologist* 'calls him "a guiding force in American archaeology for nearly half a century," excavated in 1945 and believed the site warranted further work. Vescelius was a 15-year old intern at that Bird excavation and Bird was also instrumental in getting Vescelius the 1955 excavation.

Whether or not Vescelius overlooked artifacts of prehistoric age, there is no way to reexamine the artifacts - Early Sites lost track of the 8,000 artifacts after the excavation. This leaves Vescelius's report as the sole source of information on the excavation, and that report is not helpful. Even peers had problems with Vescelius's documentation, or more specifically, lack of documentation. "Unfortunately, Vescelius had difficulty in writing up his findings and his output was limited to a few short reports and book reviews." This quote from *Andean Past* demonstrates the schism between professional and amateur archaeology. Vescelius' nonexistent documentation is "unfortunate," - the same scholars would flay alive an amateur excavator at Mystery Hill doing the same. So-called professional archaeologists may scoff at William Goodwin and his amateur fieldwork, but there is more documentation from his excavations than from that of the trained professional Vescelius.

The Early Sites group was unimpressed by Vescelius's report, and would continue to conduct their own research, but their momentum had been lost. Malcolm Pearson could now discuss leasing the site to with Bob Stone.

In 1956, Bob Stone and Malcolm Pearson signed a contract that allowed Bob Stone to lease the site for a 5-year period with an option to buy. Bob formed a corporation with several of his fellow engineers at Western Electric, bought an adjacent parcel with access to the road, leveled the parking lot, constructed a visitor's center and in the spring of 1958, Mystery Hill Caves opened to the public. Although it received a steady stream of visitors and publicity, those first five years were almost the last. Only Stone's single-minded devotion to his work kept the site afloat. Things appeared so bad that Pearson, at the end of the 5-

year lease, would only agree to a one-year extension. Mystery Hill ("Caves" had now been dropped from the advertising) limped along, as a second, then a third one-year lease extension was signed. During the third such lease, Stone realized those lease negotiations were distracting him from research. Stone took out a loan and purchased the site outright.

The lease negotiations were not the only factor involved. Bob Stone, suspecting that the acre of stone ruins were only the focal point of a larger complex, had quietly begun purchasing adjoining acreage. By the time he was done, Bob Stone and his corporation owned more than 100 acres of the hilltop. In retrospect, Stone's instincts had been impeccable. Had he waited even 10 years, rising real estate costs would have prohibited such wide scale purchases. Robert Stone's instincts had saved features he could not yet imagine - Indian cliff shelters, quarry sites, and the sprawling stone walls with carefully positioned rocks that would be discovered to be the astronomical calendar.

This brought Bob Stone and his Hill into the mid 1960's. Now free to concentrate on research, Bob and a team of dedicated volunteers began uncovering a string of discoveries that continues unabated to this day. The mid 1960's were also the time when Alexander Thom and Gerald Hawkins began publishing their respective works on possible mathematical and astronomical aspects of British megalithic sites such as Stonehenge. Bob Stone had already begun to focus on the large standing stones in the walls circling the site as being more than decorative. With Hawkin's *Stonehenge Decoded* making headlines, Stone decided to take a closer look.

Goodwin had also known of these stones, but dismissed them as construction blocks being "cured" when the site was abandoned. And since they weren't on his property, they were of no concern to him. They were, however, on Bob Stone's property. If these monoliths had astronomical alignments attached to them, Stone reasoned that the most westward-situated stone would mark the farthest point along the horizon that the sun moved - the midwinter solstice. It seemed simple enough in theory: if the monolith did indicate the Winter (Hibernal)

Solstice, then anyone standing in alignment with the center of the site on that date would see the sun set directly behind the stone.

By 1967, Stone's research was concentrating on the primary solar alignments: Hibernal Solstice, Vernal Solstice and Equinox. There were three problems however. First, no one knew where the center of the site was, making it impossible to determine the alignment. Secondly, there was 50 years of forest growing between the acre of stone ruins and the monolith. Many hours of timber clearing finally allowed an unobstructed view of the horizon behind the suspected solstice stone. And third, New England weather in December can be unpleasant and unpredictable - Bob had yet to actually verify the sun setting behind the winter solstice sunset monolith.

Bob Stone, while searching the walls for other monoliths, discovered a large one pointing due north. Putting this North Stone in alignment with the stone ruins, Bob found that this monolith bisected the acre of stone ruins. More important, with a north to south line to work from, he could calculate a logical place for the winter solstice sunset to intercept that line, giving him the center of the site. What he discovered was that the center of the site was the sacrificial table, or very close to it. The problem, it would turn out, was still the weather.

For three years, Bob Stone struggled a mile from the road through waist deep snow to wait for sunset, only to see it obscured by clouds. Finally, in 1970, the weather held. It was a beautiful colored sunset. Bob used a complete roll of film, shooting a series of photographs of the sun setting behind the winter solstice marker, including the one used on the cover of this book.

The North Stone aligns with Thuban 3600 BC to
1700 DC *(David Goudsward Photo)*

Summer Solstice Sunrise (top) and Sunset (bottom) monoliths mark longest day of the year, approximately June 21 on the current calendar. (Photos are not to scale. *David Goudsward Photos*)

With proof that there were astronomical alignments, Bob's cousin, Osborn Stone, was put in charge of the ongoing astronomical investigation. An engineer and pilot with some experience in surveying techniques, Oz Stone and a team of volunteers were able to locate and verify 18 distinct solar and lunar alignments. By 1973 however, it was becoming increasingly clear that the sheer scope of the project would require a complete survey of the site.

In 1977, B.V. Pearson Associates, a local survey firm, was contracted to survey relative distances among all site features and to verify the property lines. Surveyor Charles Pearson, Bob Stone, and Oz Stone coordinated the project. The Pearson survey confirmed that there were numerous stone walls that did not align with any boundary line, current or historical. Additionally, the stone walls didn't conform to Colonial stone wall appearance or construction. In 1987, in a letter written in response to a brief but wildly inaccurate television spot on the site, Charles Pearson reiterated the differences, adding,

> ... *it is obvious that the major standing stones we have located were placed to indicate many of the significant astronomical events of the sun and moon, and it is difficult for us to imagine anyone reviewing the physical evidence at the site and on our survey plan and reaching any other conclusion. This is not astronomical theory, but a straightforward geometrical analysis of measured fact at the site...*

The survey's verification of the north line was considered a priority. With that data, the age of the site could be calculated by determining at what point in the earth's precession the stone aligned with which North Star.

Precession, or more properly, Precession of the Equinoxes, is the westward motion of the equinoxes. It also causes a circular rotation that changes which star is the North Star as seen from Earth. Slowly, the Earth's North Pole traces a circle in the sky, and the appearance is of stars moving in and out of alignment. Thuban was the pole star while the Egyptians built the Pyramids in Egypt. The motion of precession rotated the Earth's axis away from Thuban toward Polaris, the current pole star. In a few centuries, there will be no North Star as Polaris moves out of alignment. In 6000 years, Deneb will be North Star and 13,000 years from now, Earth's rotation will point north at Vega.

The rotation of the Earth makes the planet behave like a top or gyroscope spinning in space. If the Earth were a perfect sphere, then the rotation axis would remain pointed in the same direction all the time, like a gyroscope. However, the Earth is not perfectly spherical - it is made of an uneven distribution of rocks and water, which is covered by a layer of fauna, flora, and air. Neither is the Earth's crust, though made of rock perfectly stiff, and the extremely fast rotation causes the planet to flatten slightly at the poles and bulge at the equator. This squashed sphere effect is called an oblate spheroid and it makes the equatorial diameter of the Earth about 43 km larger than the polar diameter. This equatorial bulge throws the planet out of alignment with the gravitational forces exerted by the Sun and Moon. The planet, in effect, wobbles in its orbit. One complete wobble takes 26,000 years.

By determining the alignment of the North Stone, the date of the site's construction can be narrowed down. A further clue was two small stones on either side of the North Stone. These smaller stone were placed as if to mark a 5-degree arc of movement. This inferred a North Star that was not true north, and moving across the night sky.

Oz Stone calculated the movements of the current and former North Stars, Polaris and Thuban, and determined that either one fit in terms of alignment, including the 5-degree factor. Thuban between approximately 3600 BC and 1700 BC, and Polaris after 1450 AD both matched the data. So, based only on Pole Star alignment, the site was built between 3600-1700 BC or after 1450 AD.

A construction date after 1450 AD can immediately be discarded. Astronomy did not gain popularity with the general public in America until the second half of the 19th century - the Pattee family would have been extremely unlikely to know of precession, never mind sufficient information to accurately mark the traverse of the North Star as it was in a previous century. Goodwin may have had access to such information, but disregarded the standing stones as unimportant. Additionally, his 9th century Culdee theory would not be supported by any date suggested by the alignment.

This leaves the window of 3600 BC to 1700 BC. This 1900-year period could be narrowed by another avenue of research that had shown results on other archaeological sites - radiocarbon dating.

There are three isotopes of carbon which occur naturally - C12, C13 and C14. Of these three isotopes, C12 is the most common form and C14 is the rarest. One carbon 14 atom exists in nature for every trillion C12 atoms in living material. Radiocarbon dating is based on the rate of decay in these radioactive unstable C14 isotopes.

C14 is formed in the upper atmosphere when cosmic rays strike nitrogen atoms. The C14 joins with oxygen atoms to create carbon dioxide. Plants in photosynthesis then utilize the carbon dioxide. Herbivores eat the plants, and carnivores eat the herbivores. C14 is distributed throughout the food chain. When a plant or animal dies, it obviously stops eating. There is no further replenishment of radioactive carbon, only the steady decay of the C14.

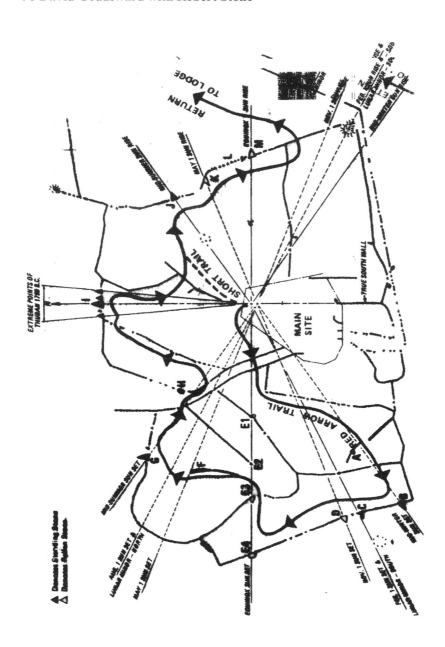

In 1948, Dr. Willard Libby first discovered that this decay occurs at a constant rate. His research found that after 5568 years, half the C14 in the original sample will have decayed and after another 5568 years, half of that remaining material will have decayed, and so on. The half-life is the name given to this value, which Libby measured at 5568±30 years. This became known as the Libby half-life. After 10 half-lives, there is a very small amount of radioactive carbon present in a sample. At about 50 - 60,000 years, then, the limit of the technique is reached. By measuring the C14 concentration in a sample, it is possible to calculate the age of the sample.

Anything with a carbon base is measurable: bone, shell, paper, leather, mud soil, ice, pollen, hair, wood, pottery, even cave paintings. But the best sample material is charcoal. Since the inception of the dating technique in the 1950's, charcoal has been acknowledged as the most reliable material for dating. Charcoal and wood are fairly sturdy, so the sample can be more rigorously cleaned of contaminants without destroying the sample.

C14 dating is not exact. There is still ongoing debate as to the half-life duration. Later measurements of the Libby half-life indicated the figure was 3% too low and a more accurate half-life was 5730±40 years. This is known as the Cambridge half-life. (To convert a "Libby" age to an age using the Cambridge half-life, multiply by 1.03).

Radiocarbon dating had been used successfully on the hill in August of 1967 when Bob Stone and a team of researchers excavated a pine stump that was sufficiently intact to date. Geochron Laboratories in Cambridge, Massachusetts was sent a sample suitable for testing. The date returned was 260 +/- 90 C14 years BP (before present), or a time frame of 1600-1780 with a median of around 1690. This is a significant date, in that the pine stump tested had roots that had grown into a chamber wall. Since the chamber had to be there prior to the tree for the roots to penetrate the wall, this eliminated Jonathan Pattee as builder. It doesn't eliminate the earlier family members on the property, who arrive in the 1730's, but it further invalidates the

Vescelius and Hencken conclusions. It didn't help pinpoint who actually build the structure or when it was built, but a further clue was forthcoming from the soil beneath the stump.

In 1969, amateur archeologist James Whittall sank a 32" by 42" trench alongside the pine stump to discover whether the structure was built on bedrock, and what artifacts might be left from that construction. The excavation found three distinct layers of soil. The first 5 inches were topsoil leading to a second level of reddish soil, 11 inches deep. In these first two levels, Whittall found colonial and post colonial artifacts - buttons, hooks, eyeglass frames and pottery. This was expected and it just confirmed use by the Pattee family over a period of time.

The third level proved to be enlightening. The yellow soil ran 10 inches down to bedrock. The color matched the glacial clays surrounding the hill, inferring this was windblown accumulation over a large period of time. The first 3 inches were sterile soil - no evidence of disturbance. Then, Whittall hit pay dirt. In the next three inches, he uncovered a hammer stone, a scraper and quarrying spalls - evidence of someone working with stone beside this structure long before English settlements in the region. How long was unknown, until Whittall continued down a fraction of an inch and uncovered flakes of charcoal.

The reports came back with a date that confirmed Bob Stone's instinct - 2995 years before present +/- 180 years. In 1000 BC, someone was on Mystery Hill using stone tools. Whittall would continue through another 3 inches of sterile yellow soil before reaching bedrock and prove the structure was resting on the bedrock. Since there were roughly 24 inches of soil between surface and 3000 year-old charcoal, it is safe to estimate that soil accumulated in that vicinity at the rate of approximately 1 inch per 125 years.

Since 3 inches of soil has accumulated from the time the first stone in the foundation was laid until the stone tools were dropped, approximately another 375 years can be added to the construction date. Whittall had found proof that this chamber was built more than 3000 years ago.

Bob Stone was elated, but realized he had more questions than answers. Astronomical work was suggesting a date still older than the carbon-14 dates had proven. He needed to continue to search for evidence to confirm one date or another. He needed a date to determine which cultures in that time period possessed the stone working and astronomical skills to build the site. While excavations and alignment surveying went on, attention was turned to comparative archaeology.

Comparative archaeology is the attempt to identify an unknown culture based on similarities to a known culture. It is at best an inexact science. The problem is that even if you find a culture with similar aspects, you must determine if it is due to diffusion or parallelism. In other words, did one culture influence the development of another, or did the two cultures remain isolated from each other, developing similar traits by coincidence.

For instance, astronomical alignments by themselves are not an uncommon cultural development. The celestial bodies in the sky have a finite cycle of repetition. Any culture that observes the skies will note the same patterns and repeating phenomena — solstices, equinoxes, eclipses, etc. Just because Britain's Stonehenge and Casa Grande in New Mexico both mark the summer solstice does not infer that the two cultures had any contact.

One of the earliest researchers on the site was Frank Glynn, a well-respected amateur archaeologist who had served as president of the Archaeological Society of Connecticut. Glynn approached Mystery Hill from a different perspective. He believed the question of who built the site could be determined by understanding the functional of the structures. As such, Glynn devoted a great deal of time drawing comparisons between Mystery Hill and European stone structures. Although Goodwin coined the term 'sacrificial table,' Glynn assigned names to other features as he interpreted their use. Glynn's names, coined in the mid 1950's as his affiliation with Bob Stone began in earnest, reflected his theories. So pervasive were Glynn's interpretations that even now, 40 years later, these names are the terms used in the tour guides and in research notes. Glynn was part of the team that excavated the pine stump root that predated the Pattees on the site. He also participated in the early excavations of the watch house, which help lead to a greater understanding of the masonry techniques used in construction. It was Glynn who uncovered the shallow stone stairs into the Pattee cellar hole, a positive indication that the Pattees modified a preexisting structure to build their home upon.

For all of his contributions to research, Frank Glynn's most lasting legacy may be that his suggestion that there might be a connection to European megalithic cultures. Glynn eventually came to the conclusion that if all the Bronze Age cultures in Europe were compared to Mystery Hill site features; the most similar culture in Europe was the megalithic culture found on the three tiny Mediterranean islands of Malta. In 1955, Glynn drew up a preliminary article noting some of the parallels between North Salem and Maltese sites, particularly the temple at Hal-Tarzien. His observations included such items as altar slabs and oracular tubes, size and shape of small cells, walled in spaces that are open to the sky and chambers covered by stone corbelled and slab roofs.

In 1967, barely a year before his death, Glynn learned that a fellow researcher, James Whittall, was going to Europe to study megalithic structures firsthand. Glynn discussed his theory with Whittall, who agreed to pursue the matter while in Europe. Whittall compared the parallels Frank had pointed out while at Hal-Tarxien, Hagar Qim and other Maltese sites. Whittall noted additional parallels, such as drains carved into the bedrock and a construction technique where orthostats (large stone slabs, set vertically in a structure) are filled in with rubble. However, Whittall also noted similarities between North Salem and the northwestern part of the Iberian Peninsula.

Whittall stated, "The most unique parallel I noticed was the stone walls. In all my travels throughout the Western Europe and Mediterranean area I found these uniquely different walls only in one area. This was in Northern Portugal within twenty miles of the Duruo River in the provinces of Minho and Traz-os-Montes. These walls were related to the ancient Celtic hill-top settlements located throughout the Northwestern Iberian area."

Whittall noted an additional number of common traits between Mystery Hill and Portuguese locations such as Citania de Briterros and Castro de Sabrosos. However, the similarities in Malta and the similarities in Portugal were not comparable with each other. Whittall already had conducted numerous excavations on Mystery Hill and had recovered sufficient charcoal for carbon-14 testing from several locations. These carbon-14 results showed 2000 BC and 400 BC results. Based on this range of dates, in tandem with the distinctively different parallels from Europe, Whittall concluded that Mystery Hill had two ancient occupations - settlers from Malta followed by occupants from the northwestern coast of Iberia. There was no hard evidence to back up this theory, just the comparative styles. However, Whittall's continued research into the megaliths of Portugal and Spain were beginning to give him a growing reputation in the field. And it was because of Whittall's extensive background that a researcher who had been developing a theory of his own approached him.

In 1975, Whittall brought to Mystery Hill a researcher he had been corresponding with. Howard Barraclough Fell, Marine Biologist by profession, epigrapher by avocation, was on a quest. Barry Fell was compiling numerous instances of carvings in stone throughout New Hampshire and Vermont that he suspected of being evidence of pre-Columbian contact between the old and new worlds. This suspicion would become *America BC*, a best-selling

Jim Whittall examines artifacts on the site, 1974.
*(Malcolm Pearson photo)*

nonfiction title that features a chapter on Mystery Hill.

Fell arrived at Mystery Hill and was shown one of several flat stones that Bob Stone and Jim Whitall had found previously. Fell immediately recognized the stone has being written in Iberian Punic. After a week of study, Fell pronounced that the stone was a broken piece of a larger tablet containing eight characters of the Iberian alphabet. The language was a form of Iberian Punic used circa 600-700 BC in the southwestern part of Spain during the early part of the Carthaginian occupation. The fragment read *"walaya bi ... nahata-hu..."* It translated to "Embellished by ... hewed this stonework..."

The stone was the lithic equivalent of an artist's signature. Fell translated a second tablet as a dedicatory tablet to the god Baal in Iberian Punic. Fell advised Bob that he suspected that other structures would have been dedicated to other divinities and that other tablets were out there to be discovered.

On a subsequent visit to the site with Whittall and Dr. George Carter of Texas A&M, Fell was examining the area where the first tablet had been found when Bob Stone found another tablet, this time "dedicated to Bel" in Ogam. Fell considered this a major find. He had long hypothesized that the Phoenician god Baal was the same deity as the Celtic sun god Bel - these two New World votive tablets offered proof on the Baal-Bel connection in the Old World.

Ogham, or Ogam, is a script of 15 consonants and five vowels that use sets of parallel vertical lines to designate the positions of sounds. Visually, it looks like tally marks balanced above, below and through a horizontal guideline that may or may not be supplied.

Found by Jim Whitall in the early 70's, Barry Fell considered this to be one of the most important inscriptions found on the site. Fell identifies it as a dedicating a temple "to Baal of the Canaanites." Fell's translation of the Iberian characters indicated a possible connection between the Phoenician god Baal and the Celtic sun god Bel. *(Robert Stone Photo)*

Ogham can also run as parallel horizontal lines on a vertical stem-line. The variant found in North America is vowel less, or consaine. Ogham is an alphabet, as opposed to a language. This means in addition to variable orientation and no vowels, Ogham can also represent a number of languages.

Before 1975 had ended, another stone was uncovered; an inscribed stele that Fell believed gave an indication of the length of time the builders remained in the region. This inscribed stele, now known as "The Beltane Stone," is also written in Ogam but also has Roman numerals. It is edge-inscribed, in a style similar to that of Ogam steles found in Britain, but without vowels. Fell translated the stele as "Day 39." This was significant, Fell felt, because there was a very small window of time in which the phrase "39 days" was significant. The Celtic calendar began on the vernal equinox. When Julius Caesar introduced the reformed calendar in 45 BC, the vernal equinox was set at March 25 and the start of summer as May 8. However, in the Celtic regions, the traditional festival of Beltane on May 1 was considered the beginning of summer. By the Julian calendar, 39 days elapse between the start of the year until Beltane, which appears on the Latin Celtic calendar as Day 39. Because of precession of the equinox, the number of days between vernal equinox and Beltane has increased, meaning the Beltane Stone would have to have been inscribed around the time of Julius Caesar and the early Roman emperors. Any later, the number of days would be wrong. It could not have been inscribed earlier, because Roman numerals weren't used by the Celts until after Caesar conquered them. Combining the estimated age of the Iberian Punic with the age of the Ogam, Fell hypothesized that the site was occupied by 800 BC and remained in contact with Europe for 7 centuries until the era of Julius Caesar.

*America B.C.* and Fell's subsequent volumes immediately galvanized the academic world against Fell, his work and anything remotely attached to him. An extraordinary linguist, Fell learned Maori, Latin, French, German and Ancient and Modern Greek while still a student. While at the University of Edinburgh, he also learned Danish and spent time on the coast of northwest Scotland to learn Gaelic. Later he acquired a working knowledge of Russian, Sanskrit, Egyptian hieroglyphics and more than a dozen other languages of Africa, Asia and America. All of these skills combined to allow Fell to recognize, if not immediately translate, a variety of obscure texts. As *America B.C.* climbed the bestseller lists, Fell was inundated with new reports of mysterious epigraphic finds. Fell was unable to keep up with the onslaught. Each time he made an error in translation or translated a fraudulent tablet, his critics jumped upon it as proof of Fell's facetiousness. Fell's inability to admit to his errors and his intolerance toward critics eroded into his support. Although Fell continued to publish and translate until his death, the forward momentum of his epigraphic movement stalled against the stone walling of academic based archaeologists.

However, by Barry Fell's death in 1994, the academic stone wall was beginning to show cracks. This is not to say his work has been absolved of error and embraced, but there is hope.

One of the first was philologist David H. Kelley, author of *Deciphering the Mayan Script*, a 1976 text instrumental in establishing the phonetic character of the Mayan glyphs. In a 1990 article for *Review of Archaeology*, Kelley discusses the occurrence of Tifinaugh and Ogham on North America. Kelley makes no excuses for Fell, but points out a basic fact - Fell, flaws and all, brought North American examples of these ancient written languages to the attention of scholars. Kelley makes the point that regardless of anyone's opinion of Fell and his work, there is Ogham in North America, and agrees with Fell that this variation of Ogham appears to have originated on the Iberian peninsula - Spain and Portugal.

The Iberian Peninsula is virtually cut off from mainland Europe by the barrier of the Pyrenees. These mountains can be crossed only at their coastal edges, either west along the Atlantic, or east, along the Mediterranean. The Celtic population occupied about half of the Iberian Peninsula, with centuries of contact with Iberians in the east and Carthaginians in the south. As such, a culture developed distinctly different from the main Celtic identity, a hybrid of the Iberian and Celt culture, with Carthaginian influence. This group is identified as the Celtiberian people. It was originally used by the Greeks to denote 'those people of Iberia who are Celtic'. There is evidence that the ancestors of the Celtiberian groups were already in the Meseta area from at least 1000 BC and probably much earlier.

The Celts were a group of peoples that occupied lands stretching from the British Isles to Turkey. The people who made up these various tribes were called *Galli* by the Romans and *Keltoi* by the Greeks, terms meaning barbarian. It is from the Greek *Keltoi* that Celt is derived.

The Celts left no written record of themselves. The few observations on these tribes are from other cultures that interacted with them, mostly from the opposite side of a battlefield.

The first recorded encounter with the Celts comes from northern Italy around 400 BC, when a group of barbarians came down from the Alps and displaced the Etruscans from the Po valley. The next encounter with the Celts came with the Roman Empire. The Romans had sent three envoys to the besieged Etruscans to study this threat to the young empire. We know from Livy's The Early History of Rome that this first encounter with Rome was quite civilized, until the Romans attempted to change their own rules. The Celt response was to tear through all Roman defenses and lay siege to Rome itself. The Romans were able to ransom their freedom, but Rome never suffered a more humiliating defeat. Other Roman historians, such as Diodorus Siculus in his History, describe the Celts as demonic in appearance. Indeed, the Romans considered the Celts a major threat for centuries.

There were actually numerous small tribes of Celtic origin, as opposed to one unified nation, but there was a unifying language spoken by all the Celt tribes, cleverly called "Old Celtic." The language seems to have come from the original Ur-language and from the Indo-European language tradition. In fact, the form of old Celtic was the closest cousin to Italic, the precursor of Latin.

The original waves of Celtic immigrants to the British Isles are called the q-Celts and spoke Goidelic. It is not known exactly when this immigration occurred but it may be placed sometime in the window of 2000 to 1200 BC. The label q-Celtic stems from the differences between this early Celtic tongue and Italic. Some of the differences between Italic and Celtic include a lack of a "p" in Celtic and an" a" in place of the Italic "o." A second, later wave of Celtic immigrants to the British Isles is referred to as the p-Celts, speaking Brythonic. Goidelic led to the formation of the three Gaelic languages spoken in Ireland, Man and later Scotland. Brythonic gave us two British Isles languages, Welsh and Cornish, as well as Breton, spoken in Brittany.

Ogam was only used by q-Celts, and the 2000 BC date of their exodus from the European mainland also coincides with the carbon-14 dates at Mystery Hill. But is it actually a coincidence? There are several other intriguing points.

The first are the Portuguese and Galician "castros" - the hillforts that Whittall felt showed similarities the New England sites. The castros are located on hilltops throughout Galicia, North Portugal and parts of western Castile. They are like other European hillforts in their size and location, but use more stone in their construction and include circular and rectangular houses, flagged streets, wells and stock enclosures. Castros can be linked with the Celtic-speaking population throughout history in Iberia, but they are not the only sites to be associated with Celtic people.

In 1962, the Irish Folklore Commission published a study of the Lammas, or Lughnasa, festival, looking at how the Celtic harvest festival survived after the arrival of Christianity. What is intriguing is the reoccurring use of mountain and hilltops. In County Tyrone, on Slieve Beagh, is a glen. A steep path climbs out of the glen to an outcrop. There rests a chair-shaped rock. Near this chair is a large square stone known as the Altar. Near the Altar is another flat rock resting on boulders with a bowl shaped hollow that collects water.

The Lammas study also mentions the work of John O'Donovan, who in 1834 began visiting ancient monuments to record the local traditions about them. This body of work, known as the Ordnance Survey Letters starts out in great detail as O'Donovan explores the oral traditions. However, O'Donovan expected to retrieve information that supplemented the written texts. As the long journey into the countryside progressed, O'Donovan grew more discouraged by the seeming irrelevance of the local traditions. But when he visited Slieve Donard in County Down, it was still early in the trip, and O'Donovan not only recorded the local legends but the physical layout of the ancient site. O'Donovan, a manuscript scholar, is enthusiastic about this site because of it's mention in John Colgan's Acta Sanctorum Hiberniae (Louvaine, 1647). He described the ascent and the summit, where he found cairns and two wells, one of which was dry. To the east of the well was an altar, and indications of at least one small stone structure. O'Donovan was told of a legend of a subterranean passage that ran to the summit. The description of Slieve Donard is strikingly similar to the layout of Mystery Hill, right down to one of the wells being dry. Does this mean Mystery Hill was a Lammas Hill, used by Celtiberians?

In 1998, Pennsylvania State University Astronomy Professor Louis Winkler began to examine the astronomical alignments of the site. Not only does his work reinterpret the various alignments; it may also indicate a different construction sequence. Winkler argues that the scope of previous studies is insufficient. Although his studies focus on the 14-acre area commonly referred to as the astronomical complex, he believes the entire hilltop, some additional 90 acres of woods and stone walls, is an integral part of the alignments. New surveys of these additional walls are underway, which are more extensive than anticipated, and do not correlate with any historical property boundaries.

Winkler believes that the north-south axis was determined by bisecting the angle formed by the rising and setting of the star Sirius.

Building from this axis, midyear points could be determined, all of which intersect at the destroyed mounds in the main site. The midyear points allowed eight cardinal times of the year to be determined. Winkler points out that even this early in the construction, the site bears striking resemblance to Bronze Age sites in the British Isles, particularly Callanish in Scotland's Isle of Lewis.

Winkler's work encompasses the various walls that cross the 14 acres of the astronomical area, and he believes that the walls indicate a large variety of alignments – solar, lunar and stellar. In fact, under Winkler's interpretation, stellar alignments are the significant alignments, and notes two distinct types: zenith stars and grazing-circumpolar stars. Zenith stars pass overhead and dip below the horizon. Grazing-circumpolar stars also pass overhead, but never drop below the horizon. Both types of stars disappear as they near the horizon because of the extinction effect of the atmosphere, and the point of extinction is what alignment stones are marking.

When the site was being built, Arcturus, Alphecca and Vega were three distinctly bright zenith stars – stars with an apparent magnitude brighter than 3. Used as a measure of the brightness of an object as seen from the earth, the brighter the object, the lower the number. Winkler hypothesizes that Arcturus at a magnitude of –0.1 was the attention grabber, not only because it was the brightest, but also because it was in the same constellation as the only grazing circumpolar star with a magnitude brighter than 3, Izar. The constellation that is home to both Arcturus and Izar is Boötes, one of the constellations most widely recognized by ancient cultures. It depicts a herdsman driving a bear (Ursa Major) around the sky. The constellation is also associated with the Quadrantid meteor shower.

Winkler's work was also responsible for explaining a mysterious monolith that had been discovered in 1997. In the fall of 1997, Bob Stone and his son Dennis were showing neighbors Al and Peter Kayworth a potential quarry site outside of the main complex when Peter pointed a series of unmapped slabs fifteen feet beyond the quarry site. Initial visual examination indicated featured similar to other monoliths, but on a much grander scale. Closer examination revealed it indeed was the remains of the largest monolith on the site. The monolith, 14 feet high, had fallen over and broken into four pieces in the distant past – far enough back that the stone has been nearly entirely obscured by soil accumulation and encroaching brush. It remains hidden and undisturbed, a prime location for future research and C14 dating.

The location did not correspond with any known alignments, and it was theorized that the stone had possibly broken while still in construction and had been abandoned. Winkler's calculations indicated that the placement of the new monolith marked the position of extinction of the grazing circumpolar star Izar.

Winkler's work corresponds with the carbon dating, and may indicate a longer period of use for the site than has been previously suggested. In fact, his theory's weakness may be the length of habitation required for his proposed 3-phase construction – starting with Arcturus and Izar around 2000 BC and ending with Algenib and Deneb being the significant stars, circa 1500 AD. However, since Izar and Algenib, and Arcturus and Deneb rise and set in the same place, Winkler concedes that if the start of construction is pushed back to circa 2200 BC, most of the alignments can be explained in a shorter time period. Although Dr. Winkler died in 2001, the frontiers expanded by his work continue to generate new interpretations.

So the question again remains – does this mean Mystery Hill was a Lammas Hill, used by emigrant Bronze Age Celtiberians?

It depends on whom you ask. In the first few pages of this book, it was said that the greatest asset of this hill is also it's greatest liability - there has been so much damage in the last four millennia that no matter who you believe built the site, there is just enough physical evidence to warrant further investigation along that line. Yes, there are Celtiberian Ogam and Punic scripts found on the site. There are physical similarities to sites associated with Celts. The astronomical alignments and carbon-14 results coincide with the date of a major immigration by Celts. The Celtiberians interacted with Carthaginians, a nationality almost certain to have the skill to cross the Atlantic.

However, there is none of the ornamentation on the stones that would be indicative of Celts. The Ogam and Punic translations are controversial. Would a culture choose to use stone in lieu of metal tools to build a religious center? There are so many standing stones and walls that astronomical alignments could be found for any particular date, depending on the researcher. Between colonial farming, antiquarian excavations, earthquakes, New England weather and 40 years of visitors, the physical layout of the site has changed.

It may be Celtiberian, a colony preoccupied with surviving with no time for ornamentation. Or it could be the frame of reference of the current researchers. There is no answer yet to the question of who built Mystery Hill. But there is no doubt that under the careful scrutiny of Robert Stone, and now his son Dennis and grandson Kelsey, there will someday be a final chapter to the Mystery Hill Story – The Age of Answers.

The fallen 14-foot monolith marking the position of the extinction of the grazing circumpolar star Izar. *(David Goudsward Photo)*

# Bibliography

**Beginnings**
Spaulding, John. *Historical Relics of the White Mountains*
Mt. Washington [NH]: Published by J.H.Spaulding .1855

**Ice Age**
Antevs, Ernst. *The Recession of the Last Ice Sheet in New England*
New York: American Geographical Society. 1922

Brown, John. Untitled letter to John Cotton, appended to *A Holy Fear of God, and His Judgments, Exhorted To: In a Sermon Preach'd at Newton, November 3. 1727 On a Day of Fasting and Prayer, Occasion'd by the Terrible Earthquake That Shook New-England, on Lords-Day Night before.*
Boston: Printed by B. Green, jun. for S. Gerrish. 1727

Burke, John A. "Scientific Instrument Survey of the Gungywamp Complex,"
*Stonewatch - Newsletter of the Gungywamp Society.* Vol 13, No.4 Summer 1995

Devereux, Paul. *Earth Memory*
St. Paul, MN: Llewellyn Publications. 1992

Devereux, Paul. *Earthmind*
New York: Harper & Row Publishers. 1989

Goldthwait, Lawrence. *Clay Deposits of Southeastern New Hampshire*
(Part 15 - Mineral Resource Survey).
Concord, NH: New Hampshire State Planning and Development Commission. 1953

Hitchcock, C.H. *The Geology of New Hampshire*
Concord, NH: Edward A. Jenkins, State Printer. 1877

Oldale, Robert N. "Late-Glacial and Postglacial Sea-Level History of New England: A Review of Available Sea-Level Curves."
*Archaeology of Eastern North America.* 14, Fall, 1986

Persinger, M.A. "Possible infrequent geophysical sources of close UFO encounters: expected physical and behavioral-biological effects." In R.F. Haines (Ed.),
*UFO Phenomena and the Behavioral Scientist.*
Metuchen, N.J.: Scarecrow Press, 1979

Persinger, M. A. "Geophysical variables and behavior: XXI. Geomagnetic variation as possible enhancement stimuli for UFO reports preceding earthtremors."
*Perceptual and Motor Skills*, 60, 1985

Persinger, M.A. "Transient geophysical bases for ostensible UFO-related phenomena and associated verbal behavior? "
*Perceptual and Motor Skills*, 43, 1976

Simmons, William S., *Spirit of the New England Tribes*
Hanover, NH. University Press of New England, 1986

Soil Survey - Town of Salem, Rockingham County, New Hampshire
USDA - Soil Conservation Service. 1974

Sundeen, Daniel Alvin. *The Bedrock Geology of the Haverhill Fifteen Minute Quadrangle New Hampshire (Bulletin No. 5)*
[Concord, NH]: State of New Hampshire, Department of Resources and Economic Development. 1971

United States Geological Survey 7.5 X 15 minute Quadrangle Topographic Map

Haverhill Massachusetts/New Hampshire (42071-G1-TM-025)
1:25,000-scale metric topographic map. 1985

United States Geological Survey
Haverhill Sheet – Massachusetts/New Hampshire
1:62,500-scale foot topographic map. 1884

Fenton G. Keyes Associates. *Engineering Study and Report on
theWater Supply, Storage and Distribution System of the Town
of Salem,New Hampshire.*
unpublished, dated January 1971. copy kept at
Kelly Library, Salem, New Hampshire

***Megalithic Age***
*America's Stonehenge Tour Guide Map*
North Salem, NH: In-house publication. Various editions

Stewart-Smith, David. *Ancient and Modern Quarry Techniques*
Nashua, NH: Gamemasters Publishers Association. 1989.

Stone, R and O. "Strange Well at Mystery Hill," (Upper Well
Excavation)
    *The New Hampshire Archeologist*
    [Exeter, NH ]: December 1963

***Woodland Age***
Converse, Harriet Maxwell. "Myth and Legends of the New
York State Iroquois,"
*Educational Department Bulletin*
[New York State Museum] 15 December 1908 (Museum Bulle-
tin 125)

Curtin, Jeremiah, comp. *Seneca Indian Myths*
New York: E.P.Dutton & Company. 1923

Hewitt, J.N.B., comp. "Seneca Fiction, Legends and Myths,"

*Thirty-Second Annual Report of the Bureau of American Ethnology to the Secretary of the Smithsonian Institute.* 1910-1911

Le Clercq, Christian. *First Establishment of the Faith in New France*
  John Gilmary Shea translator
  New York: John G. Shea. 1881
Parker, Arthur C. *Seneca Myths and Folk Tales*
Buffalo, New York: Buffalo Historic Society. 1923
[rpt: University of Nebraska Press, 1989]

Price, Chester B. "Historic Indian Trails of New Hampshire," *New Hampshire Archeologist.* March 1958

Stewart-Smith, D., et al. "Mystery Hill Research Committee Report"
Mss dated 7 June 1995.

**Pattee Age**
Gilbert, Edgar. *History of Salem, N.H.*
Concord, NH: Rumford Printing Company. 1907

Harriman, Walter. *History of Warner, New Hampshire*
Warner, NH: Republican Press Association. 1879

*Haverhill* [MA] *Evening Gazette.* "Origin of Caves Cleared Up by Kin of Builder"
17 August 1934

Rothovius, Andrew E. "Wild Applause Greeted Lafayette During Course of His Extended Tour of New Hampshire"
  *Milford* [NH] *Cabinet.* 20 December 1962.

Scalisi, Marie Lollo and Virginia M. Ryan. "Peter Pattee of Haverhill Massachusetts: A 'Journeyman Shoemaker' and His Descendants"

*New England Historical and Genealogical Register* (Boston, MA). October 1992, January 1993, April 1993

Woodbury, Dr. George. "Tourists Can Take it From Here - 'Mystery Caves' - Ancient Ruins or Codger's Retreat? *New Hampshire Sunday News* (Manchester, NH). 13 July 1958

**Antiquarian Age**
Burleson. Donald R. *H. P. Lovecraft A Critical Study* Westport, CT: Greenwood Press. 1983

Chase, George Wingate. *History of Haverhill, Massachusetts* Haverhill: Published by the Author. 1861

Crowley, Aleister. "Rex de Arte Regia," edited and annotated format, in *The Magical Record of the Beast 666: the Diaries of Aleister Crowley, 1914-1920.* John Symonds and Kenneth Grant, eds. London, Duckworth, 1972.

Goodwin, Charles A. *A Brief Sketch in Remembrance of William B. Goodwin, 1866-1950.* Hartford, CT: Privately published. 1950

Goodwin, James Junius. *The Goodwins of Hartford, CT.* Hartford, CT: Brown & Gross. 1891

Goodwin, William B. Correspondence to Harral Ayres Copy on file at Mystery Hill

Goodwin, William B. *The Lure of Gold* Boston, MA: Meador Publishing. 1940

Goodwin, William B. "Notes Regarding the Origin of Fort Ninigret in the Narragansett Country at Charlestown,"

*Rhode Island Historical Society Collections*. Volume XXV, No.1, January 1932

Goodwin, William B. *The Ruins of Great Ireland in New England*
Boston, MA: Meador Publishing. 1946

Goodwin, William B. *Spanish and English Ruins in Jamaica*
Boston, MA: Meador Publishing. 1946

Goodwin, William B. *The Truth About Leif Ericsson*
Boston, MA: Meador Publishing. 1941

Goudsward, David R. *Horror on the Hill*
Nashua, NH: Gamemasters Publishers Association. 1989.

Hencken, Hugh. "The 'Irish Monastery' at North Salem, NH"
*New England Quarterly*. September 1939

Hencken, Hugh. "What are Pattee's Caves?"
*Scientific American*. November 1940

Humphrey, Richard V., ed. *The Mystery Hill Source Book 1907-1945*
Salem, NH: Teaparty Books. 1979

Hunt, William R. *North of 53 - The Wild Days of the Alaska-Yukon Mining Frontier 1870-1914*
NY: MacMillan Publishing Co. 1974

Judge, Joseph. "Our Search for the True Columbus Landfall"
*National Geographic* (Washington, D.C.) November 1986

Lovecraft, H.P. "The Dunwich Horror"
*The Best of H.P. Lovecraft: Bloodcurdling Tales of Horror and the Macabre*
New York: Ballantine Books. 1982

[n.b. various editions available]

Morison, Samuel Eliot. *Admiral of the Seas*
Boston: Little, Brown & Company. 1942

Morison, Samuel Eliot. *The European Discovery of America:
Northern Voyages A.D. 500-1600*
New York: Oxford University Press. 1971

Morison, Samuel Eliot. "The Route of Columbus Along the
North Coast of Haiti and the Site of Navidad."
*Transactions of the American Philosophical Society (*new ser.,
v. 31, pt. 4), 1940

Munn, H. Warner. Correspondence to Donald R. Burleson, 7
February 1979
Original owned by Donald R. Burleson.

National Geographic. "Navidad"
(Washington DC) November 1987

Pattee, Fred Lewis. *Pasquaney: A Study*
Bristol, NH: [private printing]. 1893

Portors, Frank. "Problem for Archaeologists"
*Haverhill* [MA] *Evening Gazette.* 15 Aug 1934

Robbins, Roland and Evan Jones. *Hidden America*
New York: Alfred A Knopf - Borzoi Book. 1959

Siebert, Wilbur. "The Underground Railroad in Massachusetts"
*Proceedings of the American Antiquarian Society.* Volume 45.
Part 1 (New Series). 1935

Strandwold, Olaf. *Norse Runic Inscriptions along the Atlantic
Seaboard*
[published by the author], Prosser, WA, 1939.

Wroth, Lawrence C. *The Walpole Society - Five Decades*
The Walpole Society. 1960

***Stone Age***
Burger, Richard L., and Thomas F. Lynch. "Gary S. Vescelius
(1930-1982)"
*Andean Past. Volume 1, 1987*

Castle, Peter H J . "Howard Barraclough Fell" (obituary)
*Yearbook of the Academy Council of The Royal Society of New
Zealand, 1996*

Dexter, Warren W. *Ogam Consaine and Tifinag Alphabets*
Rutland, VT: Academy Press. 1984

Diodorus Siculus. *History.*
C.H. Oldfather, editor.
London: 1933

Feldman, Mark. *The Mystery Hill Story*
North Salem, NH: Mystery Hill Press. 1977

Fell, Barry. *America B.C.*
New York, NY: Simon & Schuster. 1976

Fell, Barry. *Bronze Age America*
New York, NY: Little Brown & Company. 1982

Fell, Barry. *Saga America*
New York, NY: Times Books. 1980

Fell, Barry. "The Romano-Celtic Phase at Mystery Hill, New
Hampshire, in New England"
*Occasional Publications of the Epigraphic Society.* Volume 3,
Number 54, September 1975

Filip, Jan. "Early History and Evolution of the Celts: The Archaeological Evidence."
*The Celtic Consciousness* (Symposium Papers), Robert O'Driscoll, editor.
New York, NY: George Braziller. 1982

Geochron Laboratories. Correspondence to Robert Stone et al, concerning analytical work
(Radiocarbon age determination). Unpublished.
Various dates 1967-1995

Glynn, Frank. "Some Parallels For the North Salem Site's Architecture"
Unpublished article. April 1955
(On file with Mystery Hill)

Harriman, Walter. *History of Warner, New Hampshire*
Warner, NH: Republican Press Association. 1879

Hawkins, Gerald S. Stonehenge Decoded.
NY: Dell Publishing, 1965.

Hennessy, William G., "North Salem Mystery"
*New Hampshire Profiles*. August 1952

Herm, Gerhard., *The Celts.*
NY: St. Martin's Press. 1975

Kelley, David H., "Proto-Tifinaugh and Proto-Ogham in the Americas"
*Review of Archaeology. Spring 1990.*

Lambert, Joanne Dondero. *America's Stonehenge - An Interpretive Guide*
Kingston, NH: Sunrise Publications. 1996

Livy. *The Early History of Rome*

Aubrey De Selincourt, translator
Baltimore : Penguin Books, 1978

MacNeill, Maire. The Festival of Lughnasa: *A Study of the Survival of the Celtic Festival of the Beginning of Harvest.*
Oxford University Press. 1962

Moore, Patrick, ed. *International Encyclopedia of Astronomy*
NY: Orion Books, 1987

Morris, Craig. "Junius Bouton Bird" [Obituary]
*American Anthropologist*. Number 87, 1985

O'Donovan, John. "Letters containing information relative to the antiquities of the
County of Down collected during the Ordnance Survey in 1834" (typescript transcription).
Bray: 1928 (University of California copy)

Pearson, Charles. Correspondence to Robert E. Stone, 11 September 1987
  Reprinted as Appendix B in Lambert, *America's Stonehenge An Interpretive Guide*
  Kingston, NH: Sunrise Publications. 1996

Rose, Mark. "Celebrating an Island Heritage"
*Archaeology Magazine*. July/August 1997

Stearns, Ezra Scollay. *Genealogical and Family History of the State of New Hampshire.*
NY: The Lewis Publishing Company, 1908.

Taylor, R.E. *Radiocarbon Dating: An Archaeological Perspective*
Boston: Academic Press, Inc. 1987

Vescelius, Gary S. "Excavation at Pattee's Caves"
*Eastern States Archeology Bulletin,* Vol 15 p.13-14 (1956)

Vescelius, Gary S. "1955 North Salem, N.H. Site Excavations"
Unpublished report to Early Sites Foundation, typescript. 1955

Wernick, Robert. "Malta's rocks of ages"
*Smithsonian.* September 1996

Whittall, II, James. "Pre-Columbian Parallels between
Mediterranean and New England Archaeology"
Abstract of an unpublished article, typescript. c.1975

Winkler, Louis and Robert E. Stone.
*Mystery Hill: It's Construction and Use 2000 BC -1600 AD.*
North Salem, NH: [published by the authors]. 1999

# Index

# AMERICA'S
## STONEHENGE:

### The Mystery Hill Story
### *From Ice Age to Stone Age*

By David Goudsward with Robert E. Stone
Foreword by Malcolm Pearson

**BRANDEN BOOKS, INC**
Boston

AUG -- '03

© Copyright 2003
Branden Books, Inc.

**Library of Congress Cataloging-in-Publication Data**

Goudsward, David.
  The Mystery Hill story : from Ice Age to Stone Age / David
Goudsward with Robert E. Stone ; foreword by Malcolm Pearson.
    p.cm.
Includes bibliographical references (p.) and index.
    ISBN 0-8283-2074-8 (pbk. : alk. paper))
    1. Mystery Hill Historic Site (N.H.). 2. Indians of North America—New
Hampshire—Antiquities. 3. Archaeoastronomy—New Hampshire. 4.
America—Discovery and exploration—Pre-Columbian. 5. New
Hampshire—Antiquities. I. Stone, Robert E. II. Title.

E78.N54 G68 2003
974.2'6—dc21                                                    9/19/2002

**Branden Books**
*Division of Branden Publishing Company, Inc.*
P.O. Box 812094
Wellesley MA 02482